L

MW01293861

In a regulated industry, you absolutely – and most certainly – need to hire a smart, knowledgeable lawyer. True, a lawyer is expensive but not hiring one could cost you time and money. While the author encourages you to read the laws and regulations for yourself, he wants you to know the rules are changing all the time. When – not if – the rules change, you could find yourself in a legal limbo of non-compliance. A smart lawyer can navigate you through troubled waters and guide you through otherwise many missteps in your journey to starting and running a legal retail cannabis dispensary.

The intent of this book is to educate and to inform. The author makes every effort to keep this publication as current as possible. However, the author makes no representations or warranties on the use of this information. Nor does he assume any liability from claims, losses or damages arising out of the use of this book. The reader should not rely on the information found in this book for any legal or professional advice. This is a guide. It is meant to educate and to inform.

With that said, do enjoy this book.

Table of Contents

About the Author

Milton Wani started Montreal's first cannabis business meetup in 2017. He believes the key to a successful and profitable business comes from building a solid reputation for consistent, quality products and offering excellent customer service. He believes that word-of-mouth is our best form of advertising, and there is nothing better said than what reflects our personal brand, our character, of who we are to each other.

Milton graduated from McGill University with a degree in accountancy, where he learned the importance of financial management and auditing in helping a business to grow. He has a graduate diploma in Technical Communications from the Algonquin College of Applied Arts and Technology, a master's in public administration from the University of Victoria, Bachelor of Arts in political science from the University of Western Ontario, and a certificate of specialization in interactive design from an online program from the University of California, San Diego.

Milton is a proud alumni member of the Sigma Chi fraternity, where he has seen young and older men grow to become leaders and community-builders. He has worked for the government of Canada as a research analyst at Human Resources and Skills Development, an evaluation analyst at Transport Canada, and a project manager at the Public Health Agency of Canada. Prior to his masters, he worked as a security guard at the American Embassy in Ottawa and as a security auditor at the British-American International Banknote Company. He also worked as a technical trainers support personnel at one of Canada's first mobile encryption and digital signature technology companies, Diversinet.

In recent years, Milton worked as an operations manager for a payment processing company, acting as a liaison with a strategic partner company's sales and customer services to serve small businesses. He volunteered for the City of Ottawa's citizen-led greenspace advisory committee, where he participated in municipal government. He later spent a summer as an organic farmer at Lanark Ecovillage, near Smith Falls, Ontario, and has a permaculture design certificate and an understanding of the soil and organic plant sciences.

Milton is exploring ideas, partnerships, and new business opportunities in the cultivation, lab testing, and extraction sides of the industry. He has spent his time building a business focused on cannabis-friendly marketing and website design with a team of developers. His future plan is to offer training to help businesses and people learn more about cannabis.

Milton has lived in Khartoum (Sudan), New Delhi (India), Ottawa, London (Ontario), Toronto, Victoria, and lives in Montreal. If you are interested in subscribing to his monthly newsletter on cannabis business news, which also offers cannabis business tips, sign up at uxbigideas.com.

Get in Touch

Opening and running a retail cannabis business is a lot of work. I want to hear from you. Connect with me online to let me know what you did or did not like about this book, and what you would like to see in the next edition. Also, feel free to tell me about your experiences in the cannabis industry.

Connect with Milton on LinkedIn: Milton accepts LinkedIn invitations from all cannabis professionals and aspiring business people. Connect at linkedin.com/in/miltonwani.

Follow Milton on Twitter: @miltonwani

What Else I do

Cannabis-friendly marketing and website design. If you need an extra hand, maybe I can help:

- Social media marketing, Facebook and Google advertising, email marketing, and search engine optimization.

- Graphic design, website design, and branding.

- Mobile responsive design, loading speed optimization, user experience A/B testing.

Do you need help navigating the compliance requirements in Canada or the United States? Maybe I can help you bring together a professional team. We leave no stone unturned. Get it right from the start and you save time and money.

Remote one-on-one meetings. I am currently working on delivering online resources to train people about the business and marketing side to startup a cannabis business. I want to tailor services to help small, medium and large organizations navigate the laws and the new changes in this evolving industry.

Acknowledgements

Every author needs a supporting cast of many who coach, critique and encourage. I am fortunate to have found that in my life. To all those listed below, let me offer you a heart-felt grateful thank you. Books are made by single authors but only get better written with help of editors and those who inspire us to do better. I thank each and every one of you.

To the readers who bought this book, it is for you that I wrote this book. People like my friend David Roy, who struggles with his own body pains and who swears he will never touch cannabis again after having a bad experience. This book has changed his mind.

Sara Cooke, a new mother, former drummer of two bands, and now editor and never-ending poetry writer, was the last editor of this book. Her love of reading started at the age of five and blossoms at nine in science fiction and fantasy. She has run a highly successful books department at Value Village for seven years and is currently writing her first historical romance novel. Sara is always editing, and I am grateful she did this book.

Christopher Handley, my graduate studies friend who gave me some of my best memories at the University of Victoria being a friend. He is also the last one to edit this book. I owe him big, and I hope he calls me for that favor.

Nathan Frechette-Gagnon is my hero. He was my first editor. He is half my present age, but more than anyone I know, I want to grow up to be just like him. He runs a successful business, Marketing Ultimum, while also a full-time student at the University of Montreal. You will never met a more driven man in your life. I am proud to call him a friend.

Nikki Chychkova gave not only her time to edit my early work but encouragements along the way. She studies computer science at Concordia University and holds an ambition to one day open up her own business. I wrote this book for people like her.

Somesh Tripathi is brains behind the search engine optimization that went into the website for this book. He owns and manages a team at Creative Web Marketers. It is a long road up, but he is well on his way to becoming a premier digital marketing agency. He is a friend and future business partner whenever I work on anything to do with digital marketing.

Larice Gabha is the wizard who shaped the website for this book. Every author needs a website genius. Larice is mine. You could never ask for a better and more communicative website developer. He is a friend first, then second, a great guy to work with.

Taayo Simmonds is my lawyer friend. He contributed his time as an editor. Without going into the details, a significant part of this book would have been missing, if it were not for his editing notes suggesting an addition. This idea itself helped to make this book richer.

Kevin Hall, CEO of International Cannabis Solutions and Executive Director of Chronic Pain Toronto, gave his time in helping to answer several basic questions in this book. He is at the forefront in working with federal, provincial and municipal governments to advance cannabis in healthcare and pain management.

Shawn Drew and Roxana Gonzalez are the powerhouse couple duo at Chronic Canvas, a cannabis photo art retail business. Both of them inspire me in so many ways. They invited me to help them at their expo booth at the Cannabis Life Conference, where I listened and learned about what it meant for them to begin a cannabis-related business.

Patricia Hopkins and Robert Williams, the wife and husband team that I have grown to love over the years for welcoming me into their family and lives. If I had another sister, it would be Patricia. If it were not for Robert, this book would not exist. He suffers from chronic back pain and he is the first cannabis 'expert' I ever met.

Antonio Bramante and Yann Lafleur deserve my gratitude. Antonio (Tony) is the Uncle of Cannabis in Montreal. If we have the 'Father' and the 'Grandfather' of cannabis in Montreal, then Tony is the 'Uncle'. He has been fighting for medical cannabis for more than 10 years, having opened one of Montreal's first medical marijuana clinics, Nature's Decision. Yann Lafleur also works tirelessly with Tony, and together they are making inroads in Montreal cannabis community. If it were not for them, the Montreal Cannabis Business meetup might not have had a place to start.

Kiran Wani is the mother of author. She does not know much about cannabis. I should also mention my sister and her son, but due to the stigma at this time, she asked that I not include her name. If it were not for the encouragements of my first cousin Renuka and her two grown up children Ishita Sehgal Sachar and Mohit Sehgal, writing this book would have felt more alone. Family is a gift, indeed.

Henry Wani, my father, who died when I was less than two-years old. I thank him for his memory and for knowing there was once a time when he held me in his arms. I aspire every day to be like him by being the best man that I can be. His spirit lives on through me and through the lives that my kindness has touched. To my family in war-ravaged South Sudan, his family, whom I may never know or see, I wish you all well.

Thank you all.

Why I Wrote this Book

I wrote this book to be a part of a change. In early 2017, I became the organizer of Montreal's first cannabis business meetup. The first. I live in a city where legalization has yet to be realized, in a province of Canada not strongly in favor of legalization. We live in a young industry with a long history. A history full of stigma and misinformed ideas that prevented us from seeing both the good and bad in marijuana. (I use "cannabis" and "marijuana" interchangeably in this book.) At the meetup, I knew many of the laws still needed to be created but I provided a forum for people to meet and to find answers. It became apparent we all still needed to learn a lot more about the basics of marijuana.

Just because people have used marijuana for more than 10 years does not make them 'experts'. You would be surprised at how few long-time users could not tell you the difference between a sativa-dominant strain and an indica-dominant one or about the health benefits of cannabis. We have all been denied our opportunity to talk openly. Now we have room to do so.

I do not claim to be an expert. A mere student. You are right to ask how it is that I can write a "how-to" book for a retail cannabis dispensary, when the fact is recreational cannabis laws are still in their infancy. You can read about my academic and government pedigree in the 'About the Author' page. This page tell you about my motivations for writing on a subject that is, frankly, far bigger than I could possibly cover. If you will let this student share what he knows, perhaps we can both be part of this change.

When I launched the Montreal Cannabis Business meetup in January 2017, I was a babe in the woods. I couldn't tell you the difference between a sativa or an indica, or what a terpene was compared to a cannabinoid – I suspect this is true for most readers. A few months later – April 13, 2017, exactly – Canada tabled legislation to legalize marijuana at the federal level for recreational use in 2018. Right around that time – April 21 to 23 – I went to the first O'Cannabiz Conference, Toronto, and I met for the first-time cannabis entrepreneurs, educators and celebrities of all kinds.

In May 2017, I went to the Cannabis Life Conference in Toronto. I joined my new friends Roxana and Shawn, who run Chronic Canvas, a cannabis photo art, retail business. Two people with a dream, making it into reality. I helped them at the booth to answer customers' questions and to give them time breaks. I met other cannabis exhibitors and learned about their businesses. I must also admit my first – not so good – dabbing experience. If I can say anything about my experiences, it is that I am no different than the scores of others who will soon follow – the new and mainstream customer.

First and foremost, I love this plant. Cannabis for me is about friendship. It is time with friends to catch up and pass a joint around. For some, it is not a choice. Medical marijuana helps people with chronic mental or physical stress and pains. I can see the health benefits in my own life.

I think most longtime cannabis users would agree there is an actual 'culture' when it comes to cannabis users. There is a joke, "People don't have to smoke pot to be 'cool', but for some unknown reason people who do, are". Cannabis has so long been in the shadows that when you meet someone else who smokes, you know you are in a private club. I hope that feeling never leaves us – of being part of a bigger family and the sense of community – regardless of all our many small differences.

I wanted to give something back. Cannabis helped me during a difficult time. I lost a job, a best friend, and a family break all around the same time. Cannabis did not solve my problems but it did help me to see that I would be okay and to forgive. Musician Melissa Etheridge and Olympic snowboarder Ross Rebagliati both said it best, "Recreational is medical".

Why did I write this book? Because I could. Having taken a single PhD. level research methods course, a masters and a business degree, it just felt natural. In this infant industry, I wanted to know what I didn't know. This is how we are all starting, so I wrote a book.

There is one less obvious reason. I live in a neighborhood that sees Main Street storefronts closed, covered with paper, and empty inside. You can also see this in other parts of the city. Early on, when the federal law was announced, I contacted my elected representatives and the local business association to meet. I wanted to share my contacts, the industry professionals that I met at the conferences and LinkedIn connections. These were CEOs, executives, law enforcement and health professional contacts, each from respectable companies and organizations. I have worked for the federal government and volunteered as a committee advisor for the City of Ottawa, so I knew what to expect.

Except for my federal representative David Lametti, who welcomed me, the rest where doors shut. A bit disheartening. I knew any real changes would have to happen at the local level. I hoped we could talk about preparing a basic plan and starting a discussion in anticipation of a future municipal public forum.

Naïve as I must be, I wanted to see our little borough in Montreal become a leader – perhaps in the world – than a follower to the cities like of Vancouver and Toronto. This is Montreal. We have a hockey team. We have to carve out a space in this industry that is distinctly Quebecois. I tip my hat to Jean Guy, a local Quebec favorite, indica strain. The heart and blood of our community is in our neighborhoods, our businesses and our jobs. I wanted to see us prosper.

Let's be honest, this book cannot give you all the answers. It is written to share what I learned about the retail cannabis business with the hope of opening doors in the minds of new readers. I am a Canadian. But I know that when the United States gets its federal house in order, Canada will be but a blip as a global competitor. Until then, let Canada be your teacher.

I also hope you can continue to use this book as a reference over the coming years.

About this Book

This book answers broad questions about how to open a retail cannabis dispensary, how much it costs, and what you have to do to run the business. Retail cannabis can also be called a "recreational, adult-use, dispensary". Keep in mind, this book focuses on the "recreational retail side" of the industry more than the "medical marijuana clinic side".

What's the difference? When you visit a medical marijuana clinic, you'll notice it looks like a doctor's office. The chairs and the waiting area. Medical marijuana patients needed a safe place to talk to cannabis with a medical and health professional. Patients previously felt unable to talk to their doctors about alternative medical treatments.

In Canada, once medical marijuana patients obtain permission from a doctor, they can receive mail-couriered, doctor prescribed, legal, safe marijuana. At present, medical clinics cannot sell cannabis in Canada. In the legal U.S. states, however, medicinal dispensaries can allow patients to smell and examine the buds before making the purchase.[1] For the medical marijuana customer, a retail cannabis stores is another place to get something different. For example, your shop might be the best place to town to CBD products with so many more choices.

Here is what you will learn:

Chapter 1: Green Rush – How to understand the cannabis industry, the cannabis laws and their implementation.

Chapter 2: The Business Plan – How to navigate the application process. Learn about the Business Plan, startup costs, sources of financing, and professionals you need to meet.

Chapter 3: Your Customers – How to understand who your customers are and what they want. Learn about the medical user, habitual user, and the new users.

Chapter 4: What Makes You Different – How to find the right business name that offers web presence appeal. Learn about key success factors that can set you apart from the competitors.

Chapter 5: The Right Product Mix – How to think of educating staff and customers about safety, and how to work with suppliers to ensure high safety standards.

Chapter 6: Menu Planning – How to think of consumer trends in planning your menu, while also thinking of style, theme, and atmosphere of your location and decor.

Chapter 7: Location and Building Layout – How to find the right place, think about your 'good neighbor' policy, and show a décor that meets your customers' needs.

Chapter 8: Security is the Cost of Doing Business – How to establish a Security Plan, cash handling procedures, cybersecurity and insurance policies.

Chapter 9: Hire, Train and Reward – How to hire trustworthy people, follow employment laws, and provide training.

Chapter 10: Marketing Your Business – How to market and promote under the current laws, learn what customers want and at what price.

Chapter 11: Web Presence – How the website and digital marketing can reach more customers. Learn social media marketing tips and about the restrictions on digital advertising.

Chapter 12: Managing Sales and Costs – How to manage inventory and control costs. Learn about the role of banks, payment processors, and point-of-sale.

Chapter 13: The Exit Plan – How to plan for when you decide to leave the business.

Our hope is to inspire you to create a place where friends come to meet and customers want to go. Our focus in this book is on building customer loyalty. Of course, there is a lot more to this book – like treating your staff with respect and gratitude – but the theme of focusing on your customers-first runs throughout the book.

Chapter 1

Green Rush

"Anyone interested in starting a cannabis business needs to be fully aware of municipal, state, and federal regulations concerning cannabis. It's far too easy to miss out on profitable opportunities and to be penalized by regulatory agencies if you're not focused on what is and isn't in line with enforced guidelines. With a space as complex and rapidly changing as the cannabis industry, lacking knowledge in this area just isn't an option."

GREG LAMBRECHT, CEO OF SINGLEPOINT, A NEVADA-BASED PUBLICLY TRADED CANNABIS HOLDINGS COMPANY

Welcome to the Green Rush! In many ways, starting a cannabis business is like starting just about any other business; except for that big, fat, hairy fact that you are about to sell cannabis. This means a retail cannabis store is not like any other business.

Of course, cannabis businesses can fail. Startup costs for getting a business license could vary from $500 to $30,000 across Canada. In Oregon, for example, a business license is $4,750 US and, if your application is rejected, a non-refundable fee of $250 US.[3] One thing is true, any mistakes you make in the process will end up costing you time and money.

Starting a cannabis dispensary requires a lot of money - more than you think. These costs include installing security monitoring systems, paying licensing fees and hiring employees – and that's just the tip of the iceberg. You may have all the skills, education and drive to create a great business, but without financing, your dream of owning a legal dispensary will not come true. Two of the most common hurdles to opening a dispensary: finding the financing and getting all the necessary permits and licenses.

What you need is a book like this to get you started!

The Future is Here

You bought this book. You probably don't need convincing why this industry is for you. Legal weed is big business. One of North America's fastest-growing industries. More than 20 percent of Americans live in states where recreational cannabis is legal and more than 65 percent live where medical cannabis is legal.[4] About five million adults in Canada now use cannabis at least once a month, which is expected to grow by 19 percent after legalization.[5] ArcView Market Research, a cannabis research firm, estimates that by 2020 about 53 percent of the legal US market will come from retail sales.[6] For the first time, 2018 could mark the year that legal retail cannabis surpasses legal medical marijuana sales. Retail cannabis could beat wine sales and give beer a run.[7] While the cannabis industry is still in its infancy, retail cannabis will continue to grow.

The Green Rush shows no sign of slowing down. ArcView Market Research reported the "U.S. market for legal cannabis grew 74 percent in 2014 to $2.7 billion, up from $1.5 billion in 2013. In 2016, the U.S. market posted $6.7 billion in revenue, up 30% from the year before. In Colorado, Washington and Oregon, where recreational use was legal before 2016, consumer spending on cannabis went up 62% between 2015 and September 2016. Estimates project a compounding annual growth rate of 25% through 2021, reaching $20.2 billion US.[8] For comparison, Deloitte Consulting reported annual sales in Canada could exceed $22.6 billion CDN in the next few years."[9]

The sudden popularity of edibles and concentrates is fueling this growth. Consumers who would never smoked cannabis are finding other methods of enjoying cannabis. The black market cannot compete with legal cannabis: consumer selection is wider, price to produce is lower, it is pesticide- and mold-free, and consumer know this.

The global demand for pharmaceutical-grade, consistent quality medical marijuana means that over the next 10 to 15 years, more countries and states will legalize. Germany, Australia, Denmark, the Czech Republic and Cyprus are all growing medical marijuana markets. Israel is a world leader in medical marijuana research, finding cures for cancer. With legal weed, comes jobs in tourism, manufacturing and sales of cannabis paraphernalia and products, the hiring of growers, lab testers, accountants, security guards and a whole host of other services.

Canada and the United States are two peas in a pod. Canada is a tenth the population size of the United States. It's best compared to California. ArcView Market Research reported "California's cannabis sales reached $2.7 billion in 2016, accounting for almost half of U.S. legal cannabis sales. Its recreational market is expected to double by 2020."[10] The Government of Ontario became the first province to declare plans to open a government-run monopoly through the Liquor Control Board of Ontario (LCBO), an approach that other provinces may also follow.

Lisa Campbell of the Toronto-based Cannabis Friendly Business Association said, "Currently the LCBO is the largest buyer of wine globally, which means they could easily be the largest buyer of weed in the near future...This has huge implications internationally as we are currently negotiating NAFTA.

Having a government monopoly on distribution hopefully means stronger trade negotiations for cannabis. Ontario and California are trade partners, so potential for future LCBO import could be enormous."[11]

A new industry is emerging in North America. "Right now, I think most of the businesses operating in the cannabis industry are small businesses," said Brendan Kennedy, CEO of private equity firm Privateer Holdings.[12] According to author Jay Currie, *Start & Run a Marijuana Dispensary or Pot Shop: Wherever it is Legal*, "The real money is in recreational marijuana."[13] Celebrities who have for years supported the open use of cannabis are now looking to take a piece of the action. Names like Whoopi Goldberg, Tommy Chong, Willie Nelson, Bob Marley family, Snoop Dog, and many others want consumers to walk into dispensaries to buy their brands. We may see the Starbucks of cannabis one day. This is our marijuana moment.

The Evolving History of Pot

You have probably heard that cannabis is a flowering plant. Cannabis has many names across the world. The ancient Hindus of India and Nepal called it ganjika. The Hindus gave cannabis to the Assyrians, who then gave it to the Scythians, Thracians, and Dacians. Ancient Greeks and Roman used cannabis. Shamans have used the drug in religious ceremonies and have done so for thousands of years. Cannabis, marijuana, weed, pot, call it what you will, but it helps people. It is hard to say when calling someone a "stoner" became a derogatory term. When cannabis went underground in the late 1930s, artists and musicians continued to smoke it. Louis Armstrong started then and did so all his life.

There is still a stigma about cannabis among doctors. Doctors do not want to be the gatekeepers. The American and Canadian medical associations has said they do not support the use of marijuana. Part of the problem is that doctors may not know the right dosage to prescribe to patients. The College of Family

Physicians of Canada released prescribing guidelines in 2014 because so many patients were asking for medical marijuana. It is difficult to find similar guidelines for doctors in the United States, although Massachusetts released its guidelines in 2013. These prescribing guidelines have provided a first step for patients and doctors.

Marijuana laws in the United States are a thorny issue. Under U.S. federal law, it is illegal to possess, use, buy, sell, or cultivate marijuana. The *Controlled Substances Act* of 1970 classifies marijuana as a Schedule I drug, claiming it has a high potential for abuse and no acceptable medical use. Some states and local governments have decriminalized cannabis to reduce the burden on the justice system from the numbers of "simple possession" offenders going to jail. Although the federal government's jurisdiction over criminal law preempts state laws, state governments have limited the enforcement of federal drug laws using the Supremacy Clause of the U.S. Constitution.

In February 2014, the Obama administration relaxed guidelines for banks to make it easier for cannabis businesses to operate like any other business. However, cannabis businesses still lack access to banks and credit unions due to Federal Reserve regulations. On August 29, 2013, the Department of Justice published the "Cole memo", which described a new set of priorities for federal prosecutors operating in states that had legalized the medical or other adult use of marijuana. This represented a significant shift for the federal government away from the strict prohibition towards a more hands-off approach, allowing states to implement their own regulatory and enforcement systems for cannabis. As of this writing, the Trump Administration is evaluating whether to rescind this "Cole Memo" from the Obama-era. California just petitioned to declassify marijuana as a Schedule I drug.

Medical marijuana research holds a promise for those with cancer, epilepsy, and dementia. The National Center for Natural Products Research in Mississippi is the only federally licensed facility in the United States to cultivate cannabis for scientific research. The Schedule I classification has hindered research. As of 2016, most cannabis-related research in the United States is on chemical components of the cannabis plant and not on the whole plant.

The involvement of the Food and Drug Administration, National Institute on Drug Abuse, and the Drug Enforcement Administration in the research approvals process has meant that medical research has not advanced much in the United States. However, the Congressional Cannabis Caucus, a bipartisan group in Congress formed in 2017, intends to increase medical research and to change regulations on banking and taxation for cannabis businesses. The caucus has taken steps to prevent the U.S. Department of Justice from using its funding to challenge states that have approved medical cannabis laws.

This is a wait and see moment.

Unlike the US where ballet boxes win state referendums, Canada won legalization through the courts. It began with decades of arrests, followed by a series of court cases between 2000 (*R. v. Parker*) and 2016 (*Allard et al v. Regina*) culminating in victories that pushed Canada's Federal government to regulate medical cannabis. In April 2017, the federal government tabled the *Cannabis Act (Bill C-45)*, following in the footsteps of the groundbreaking *2016 Task Force on Cannabis Legalization and Regulation* report. Thus beginning Canada on its journey towards legalization.

As of this writing, the retail cannabis dispensary is still illegal in Canada. The Government of Canada is waiting for parliamentary debate and discussion before its passing. The government of the day has a majority in parliament and the other parties represented have given their consents to move this proposed law forward. The time of wondering whether Canada will legalize recreational marijuana is over. It has arrived. All of the provinces, territories and municipalities are beginning to roll out their own legislation to implement new rules in anticipation of the 2018 July deadline set by the federal government.

The problem for you as a would-be dispensary owner is waiting to see how all these legalization laws will work together in your area and – more to the point – how you can get started today. Fortunately, we have eight states (Alaska, California, Colorado, Maine, Massachusetts, Nevada, Oregon, and Washington) and two cities in Canada (Vancouver and Victoria) as great references for what different jurisdictions are doing to get people started.

Know the Law

Although 20 percent of Americans live in states where recreational cannabis is legal, a lot more still needs to happen in those states to fully realize legalization. Since more than 65 percent of Americans live where medical cannabis is legal, this means that for most Americans the only legal way is for medical use.[14] Let's be clear, there is no legal way for recreational purposes in Canada either. Not yet. Only for medicinal purposes. That's it. Recreational use sales is strictly prohibited in Canada and in most of the United States.

On July 1, 2018, however, with the enactment of the federal *Cannabis Act*, Canadians will be able to possess, sell and distribute cannabis. While the federal level will decriminalize cannabis, each province can determine how to regulate the possession, sale and distribution within its own borders. This means each province can implement their own model, each slightly different from the other provinces.

Canada's *Cannabis Act* is designed "to protect public health and public safety" and in particular to:

- Protect the health of people under the age of 18 by restricting their access to cannabis,

- Protect children and others from inducements to use cannabis,

- Provide for the legal production of cannabis to reduce criminal activities,

- Deter criminal activities through appropriate sanctions and enforcement measures,

- Reduce the burden on the criminal justice system,

- Provide access to a quality-controlled supply of cannabis; and

- Enhance public awareness of the health risks associated with cannabis use.

The laws of the eight states that legalized recreational cannabis – Alaska, California, Colorado, Maine, Massachusetts, Oregon, Washington, and Nevada – have a lot in common with Canada's *Cannabis Act.* The subtle variations include:

Canada's federal, provincial and municipal governments jointly regulate cannabis. In the United States, state governments impose the rules and standards for the cannabis industry. In Canada, the federal government establishes the rules for packaging, promotion activities, standardizing potency levels and serving sizes, and tracking the sale of cannabis. There is currently no plan to share the marijuana tax revenue in Canada. The *Parliamentary Budget Officer* assumed a 60:40 split between the provinces and the federal government.[15] In the U.S., the state often shares any tax revenues raised with the cities.

Municipalities will implement provincially regulated systems. The same is true for U.S. states. Local governments will issue licenses to regulate retail locations, policing costs and bylaws around home grows.

Minimum age for Canadians to use marijuana recreationally is 18 years old. The sales, promotion, packaging, and labeling of cannabis that would appeal to those under the age of 18 is prohibited. The provinces and territories may increase the minimum age. In the U.S., this age minimum is 21.

Adults can buy or carry up to 30 grams of dried cannabis (or the non-dried equivalent), grow up to four cannabis plants per home, and make cannabis-based products at home. In the U.S., this amount is one-ounce (28.5-mg).

Recreational production will follow the system in use for medical marijuana. Health Canada needs to regulate the quality of cannabis so it is free of harmful substances. However, how "artisanal" and outdoor production will begin is still under review. In the U.S., state public health departments oversee growing quality.

Edible marijuana products will have conditions. Packaging laws will have a number of conditions to ensure the marketing of edibles to children does not happen (e.g. prohibit colourful packaging).

Unlawful sale or distribution of cannabis is punishable by up to 14 years in prison in Canada. There is no American federal equivalent to this law. Offences for possession over the 30-gram limit is subject to up to five years in prison in Canada. Additional amendments to Canada's *Criminal Code* will target drug-impaired driving.

Unlawful possession in excess of the carrying limit is a punishable offence. Offences for possession over the limit are subject to up to $100 in Colorado. In Maine, having more than 2.5-ounces can lead to a maximum sentence of 6 months in prison and fine of $1,000.

Unlawful consumption in public is punishable. Offences for public consumption is subject to a maximum fine of $100 in Alaska, Colorado, Maine and Washington, and $500 in California. Alaska is the only state that will allow the onsite consumption to a limited number of shops. Maine allows employees to have the right to re-open negotiations for smoking areas in nonpublic areas of publicly owned buildings.

Although there is a deadline set by Canada's federal government, the provinces do not have to be ready to go by July 1, 2018. In the upcoming years for Canada and the United States, you will hear more (a lot more) about the rules around packaging, testing, marketing, taxes, banking, and environmental sustainability.

How Will Legal Cannabis Be Sold?

No one can see through a crystal ball where recreational cannabis will go. Governments at all levels do have a responsibility to regulate cannabis use and to provide what is best for society. Recreational cannabis will come in three main ways:

Mail-Order System

Consumers receive cannabis directly from licensed growers by mail. Under this system, recreational users register with a licensed grower. This is how medical marijuana patients are currently doing it in Canada. This system is probably the least preferred option because of privacy concerns for mainstream customers.

Government-Run Stores

State-run liquor store systems already have an existing infrastructure. Public sector unions and national medical associations favor this approach. However, there is an initial cost to the taxpayer for opening these shops. This also means the shutting down of existing dispensaries that would now be illegal, which could lead to court challenges.

In September 2017, the Ontario government in Canada announced that recreational marijuana will be sold only at province-run stores and through a province-run website. Forty cannabis stores will be up and running by July 2018, followed by another 40 twelve months later, up to an expected 150 marijuana stores by the end of 2020. (For comparison, Ontario is home to 651 liquor stores.)[16]

Private Sector Storefronts

Consumers do enjoy a shopping experience. This approach is happening in Colorado and Washington, as well as several other states. The added benefit for governments is in stimulating the economy by drawing in private sector financing. It is also easier to implement since medical marijuana clinics already exist to fill the gap and met a lot of regulatory and security requirements.[17] Nevada, for example, is beginning by only allowing existing medical marijuana clinics to grandfather into recreational for its first 18 months of legalization.[18] This approach could also include drawing in the existing licensed producers to open their own shops, selling their line of branded products.

"One thread of our research is the degree to which people are excited about real retail. It's an indication that consumers want to be able to see it, touch it, walk around it," said Marc Solby of Lighthouse Consulting.[19] There's something natural about walking into a store and saying "hi" to staff who know you; particularly among older users who like the face-to-face contact more than buying online.

In a related study using data found in customer loyalty programs, Headset, a cannabis analytics firm based in Seattle, found that customer baskets sizes were bigger at small- and medium-size stores than at the big stores.[20] Headset believed that due to competition, the smaller stores may be providing higher customer service, resulting in more products in the basket. In other words, compared to Ontario's chain government-run model, customers might be better served by the personal touch of private-owned storefronts than the liquor store model.

What is the Cannabis Industry?

It is like drinking from a fire hose: too much in one gulp. The *Marijuana Business Factbook 2016* does a good job of breaking the cannabis industry into five distinct sectors.

- **Dispensaries and medical clinics.** Truly the face of the industry with the most customer interaction.

- **Cultivators (licensed producers).** The heart of the industry, the people who grow cannabis.

- **Cannabis infused products.** These manufacturers produce concentrates, edibles and topicals, each growing in increasing popularity.

- **Testing labs.** This is the industry's smallest sector. However, as the governments require mandatory testing, labs will continue to play a pivotal role.

- **Ancillary businesses.** These include any other businesses in the industry, such as POS software, branding and marketing services, insurance agents, accountants, and lawyers.

Government Licensed Cultivators

Becoming a licensed grower is not easy. Regulators want medical-purpose, pesticide-free and chemical-free products. They also want to reduce the affects of crime. Becoming a licensed grower is a multi-stage application process in Canada that takes more than a year to complete. Despite the hurdles, the pool of licensed growers will continue to grow to meet a national and international demand.

Cannabis Industry in Canada

Licensed Producers (LPs) are the big fish in the pond. At present, there is only 43 government-authorized producers in Canada. It's an oligopoly-like market where a few big producers set the tone along with the federal government for the entire industry. This gives Canada a lot of control over the production.

Canopy Growth is Canada's largest cultivator, supplying a third of the medical marijuana patients in Canada.[21] The company is getting ready for 2018. "This is a very big leap, in terms of our output, our capacity, our footprint," said Bruce Linton, Canopy Growth's CEO.[22] Canopy Growth is spending at least $21 million US to upgrade its Tweed Farms property with an aim of tripling its production by the July 2018 deadline.[23]

For the record, companies like Canopy Growth steer clear of the U.S. export market. There is an uncertainty of how the federal government will exercise its powers to restrict the legality of cannabis in several states. The United States is also a no-go zone for other big licensed producer, Alberta-based Aurora Cannabis. "It has to be federally legal. We've got to make sure that everything we do is kosher with the exchange," said Cam Battley, executive vice president of Aurora. "We will not touch anything in the U.S. while it's federally illegal."[24]

The one big difference between Canada and the United States is the lack of a 'craft' grower presence in the policy discussion in Canada. We may be seeing a fight brewing. Small batch, private reserve-style craft producers like Ross' Gold want a seat at the table. Craft, organic-grown Ross' Gold as a brand is best known for its founder, snowboarding Olympic gold medalist Ross Rebagliati. Ross' Gold follows all the rules for testing and labeling. But this craft producer is fighting the prevailing model "because plants and vegetables have forever been grown in facilities that don't cost $10 million and have the same security as a military base."[25]

"We'd like to see the government create a new license for craft growers and we'd like to be a part of that option so that the issue doesn't end up in the Supreme Court, which is where it will end up," said Rebagliati.[26] Cannabis Growers of Canada supports growers like Ross' Gold because they see the opportunities "craft" growers offers for drawing in tourism like the wine or brewery industry does.[27]

Most consumers appear to agree. In a study by Canadian Marc Solby of Lighthouse Consulting, about 60 percent of respondents said they would rather buy from a smaller company than big marijuana, which suggests a market for smaller "craft" producers.[28] There's a feeling among some aficionados that big business, no matter how well intentioned, is in it for the money and much less the joy of the plant and the culture that spawned the industry. That big pharma, because of its association with addicting and overprescribing medications, does not and should not represent cannabis. That cigarette companies are merchants of death. That big license producers produce stale flavored strains and – like wine for those who understand 'terroir' – that better flavors can come from special growers who love the plant and the soil it grows in.

The trajectory for Canada's licensed cultivators will only grow. Canada needs more quality-produced cannabis for domestic and international markets. Security expert David Hyde said, "I see a few hundred producers in a variety of shapes and sizes across this country, whether you've got the smaller ones who are very artisanal or craft and have got a certain angle or play, whether there's a whole raft of them who are wholesaling, who are white labeling and really are experts at the sale side or the distribution side."[29]

Cannabis Industry in the United States

In the United States, this conversation is a little different. The role of the federal government is more measured and mute. The federal government shows little favor for legalization, although eight states have legalized cannabis and several more show signs of legalization in future ballot measures.

Ironically, the federal prohibition that blocks the cannabis industry on the national level is also shielding the country's state-sanctioned cultivators from Canadian competition.[30] Most of the licensed growers in Canada are well-capitalized and more experienced giants compared to their American counterparts. Alaska, California, Colorado, Maine, Massachusetts, Oregon,

Washington, and Nevada are each walking their own paths when it comes to managing and regulating legalized cannabis. But federal oversight would go a long way in harmonizing practices.

California is an interesting example. There's a 'conservative estimate' that California grows about 13.5 million pounds of marijuana a year but consumes about 2.5 million pounds – that's almost seven times more grown than is consumed.[31] "Here's the irony: there will be a huge oversupply of product and a shortage of regulated product...We are looking at a unique situation where there's a boatload of product and a lot of folks aren't going to make it into the market," said Hezekiah Allen, executive director of the California Growers Association.[32] California's many small- and medium-size craft producers will continue to be a major exporter – legal or otherwise – to the other states.

Journalist Thomas Fuller of The New Yorker found that many California farmers preferred to stay in the black market. "It is estimated that only about 11 percent of growers — about 3,500 of 32,000 farmers in Mendocino, Humboldt and Trinity counties — applied for permits. Most farmers are deterred by the paperwork to obtain a permit, the fees and the taxes, see the penalties as light, and the need for testing and environmental standards as unnecessary."[33]

That's a problem. A crime problem. David Eyster, Mendocino's district attorney, said, "the surge marijuana business brought with it violent crime. Among the cases he is handling are a robbery and slashing death of a grower; the murder of a man at a marijuana farm by a co-worker wielding a baseball bat; an armed heist in a remote area by men who posed as law enforcement officers; and a robbery by two men and a juvenile who were invited to a barbecue and then drew guns on their hosts and fled with nine pounds of marijuana."[34]

It's also a problem for quality. In October 2016, California-based Steep Hill Labs found "residual pesticides in 84 percent of cannabis tested over a 30-day period, worrying since this was during the peak harvest time. At the December 2016 Emerald Cup, almost 17 percent of entries (including 25 percent of concentrate entries) were found to have banned pesticides, bacteria, and mold. California has a dirty cannabis problem."[35]

Said again, having a strong state-run – if not federal-run – regulation and enforcement system on cultivation is invaluable for an entire industry.

Cannabis Industry's Little Secret

For governments to ensure the quality of products remain consistent and labels accurate, quality control and lab testing are essential. The popularity of vaping and edibles will push consumer demand for responsibly manufactured, pharmaceutical-grade cannabis.

Medical and recreational users will want to receive the health-benefits promised from what's written on the terpene and cannabinoid profiles. Cannabis label laws everywhere require that all product show THC levels and that those products remain mold- and pesticide-free. Cannabis oil extract can reach 80 percent or more active THC.[36] People want to know what they buy is what they get. When all is said and done, realize that lab testing is a pillar for an entire industry.

The problem is that when it comes to lab tests, it is difficult to sustain the same level of quality by the time a customer buys the product. Cannabis flower and oils are like any other organic, once living, plant material; eventually and over time, air, humidity, temperature and light all work to degrade its potency. Controlling for these variables prolong its shelf life. That's normal. What's really the problem is the testing itself. There simply is no unified testing instrument, sample technique or quality control testing standard. What makes this harder is that lab testing is also expensive.

In 2017 March, three class-action lawsuits were filed against Canada's licensed producers over contaminated medical marijuana. Journalist Grant Robertson reported that a "Nova Scotia man said he became ill and unable to keep food down after taking regulated medical marijuana. In another case, a group of veterans became bedridden, stricken by nausea and suffered bouts of 'scary' breathing difficulties, among other symptoms."[37] These and a growing list of other incidents raised questions about the Canada's ability to enforce the industry's testing practices.

The problem is that not all labs are created equal – and, as a result, labels can be wrong. Garyn Angel, CEO of Magical Butter, an infuser machine company, said that different testers give different results.[38]He believes the problem is there are no standard operating procedures for testing marijuana and infused products. At its core, the problem is that labs do not want to share their proprietary methods because of the competition among labs.[39]

Part of the problem is that cannabis consumers equate higher THC levels with better effects, and are willing to pay higher prices. Cannabis producers know this is not exactly true. THC potency depends more on the 'entourage effect' of a combination of cannabinoids and terpenes in a strain than it does on THC percentage levels. Despite this truth, producers feel an incentive to show higher THC levels to get higher sales.

Lab testing is expensive, and labs know this too. Some testing machines cost $600,000 to buy and the staff scientists hired to run them are well-paid. From the labs' point of view, if customers are coming into the lab for only two sample tests at $100 each, where is the profit? Labs feeling the pinch of competition among competitors who can all basically do the same things may feel the need to promise more.

American executive vice president of Diagnostic Lab Corporation, Dylan Hirsch, said, "Many of the labs will sometimes say they can get better results. It can be so subjective for results on THC."[40] While most licensed producers are willing to pay extra to deliver quality-level products, some less scrupulous businesses may shop around for labs that can promise better results.

The transparency of lab testing practices in not all that much talked about in Canada's news. Solomon Israel of CBC News reported that CEO Bruce Linton of Canopy Growth did apologize in 2017 to customers for the Mettrum recall and said his company had improved its quality control practices. Canada's Aurora Cannabis also announced new disclosure rules for its third-party quality control testing, which they says will assure clients of the purity of its product.[41]

Canada and eight American legalization states are establishing standards for manufacturing that include labeling, recall measures, packaging, potency and laboratory testing for mold spores and pesticides, which could become the models for other jurisdictions. "These new standards provide the necessary protection from liability for growers, manufacturers and dispensaries. What is more, the standards ensure safer cannabis products for consumers," said Michael Aberle, national director, MMD Insurance Services.[42]

Take Action

Starting a business is hard work. You are about to enter a new industry. The following should give you a few ideas on what you can do to get started:

- **Search** online for retail cannabis dispensaries near you or in other locations to see what they offer. Get a feel for what stores look like and what they offer.

- **Read** the cannabis laws in your jurisdiction, if available, and keep up to date on the rules and laws. Go to government websites related to cannabis laws.

- **Wait** for the local regulations to set up before making any big investments. Draft guidelines and regulations will take months before finalizing. For example, if you buy an empty storefront hoping to open as a retail store, you could discover that local zoning bylaws will restrict where you can open.

- **Participate** in local government public meetings and voice your concerns. You can talk about tax regulations, zoning, business restrictions, and public safety. Now is the time to speak up on how any changes could affect you and your future business.

To prosper in a retail cannabis business, you need a complex blend of passion, vision and business acumen. It is time to think of drafting a Business Plan.

Chapter 2

The Business Plan

"Before forming a cannabis company, I'd strongly recommend that any would-be entrepreneurs consider re-evaluating their capital models including how much capital is required to start their business. The industry is bound by a wide range of changing rules and regulations, which can often lead to unforeseen hurdles and expenses – a fund set aside for unknown/unpredictable expenses should be larger than one for a non-cannabis company."[43]

ALEJANDRO CANTO, OWNER OF DIEGO PELLICER WASHINGTON, A SEATTLE-BASED UPSCALE CANNABIS DISPENSARY

Despite how it looks, a cannabis business can fail. The most common reasons include the lack of financing and the inability to get all the necessary permits. The problem for you – right now – is keeping up with all the changes happening in your jurisdiction with legalization (e.g. how far away does your shop need to be from a school?).

"All ships rise in a high tide," is a popular saying among economists. It means in a rapidly growing economy, all good and badly run businesses look like they are prospering. But no matter how good your sales and profits look, you might actually be losing money through high costs and losses. We become converts to doing things better when times get tough. Asking good questions at the start is part of writing your Business Plan. No one plans to fail, but you can plan for success.

The Application Process

Each state (province) will have its own application process and requirements. However, despite differences, there is a certain amount of consistency. The City Inspector is the local government public authority responsible for exercising autonomous authority over cannabis businesses in the area. Their job is to make sure that cannabis businesses follow the rules. As a new industry, state (provincial) and municipal procedures for cannabis businesses will continue to change as government regulators fine-tune their monitoring activities. Dispensaries will need to keep up with all the updates and do everything by the book. No shortcuts!

Be warned, if the City Inspector does not believe your application has merit and it is in the public interest to do so, he or she will reject your application. In Canada, there is the *Cannabis Act*. In United States, there are similar laws in states where recreational cannabis is legal. Your application can be rejected for the following reasons:

- Risk to public health or safety, including the risk of cannabis diverted to an illicit market or activity.

- False or misleading information submitted in the application.

- Security clearance refused or cancelled.

Because the *Cannabis Act* is federal in Canada, federal laws must also be adhered to as well (the same is true for states in the U.S.):

- Applicant violated the provisions of the *Cannabis Act*, the *Controlled Drugs and Substances Act* or the *Food and Drugs Act* in the past 10 years.

- Applicant is a young person, an individual who is not ordinarily resident in Canada, or an organization incorporated, formed or otherwise organized outside Canada.

In states where recreational cannabis is legal, applicants are required to follow existing state cannabis law, federal drug laws, and food and safety laws, where applicable. In Colorado, for example, there is a two-year residency rule for applicants. Pennsylvania's medical marijuana application process is based on several pass-fail criteria, such as proof of a clean criminal history, sufficient capital, capacity to operate, and tax clearance.[44]

In the City of Victoria, this process takes six- to eight- months from the time of submission. In other jurisdictions, this process could take longer. City of Victoria license application requires:

- Security Plan,

- Police information checks for the applicant and every on-site manager,

- Proof of a security alarm contract,

- Proof of ownership or legal possession of the premises (written consent of landlord if leased),

- Video surveillance cameras must be installed and monitored,

- Security and fire alarm system must be installed and monitored at all times, and

- Valuables must be removed from the business premises or locked in a safe on the business premises at all times when the business is not in operation.

To read more about the application process, go to the City of Victoria *Cannabis Businesses* website and Vancouver's *Regulations for medical marijuana-related businesses* website.

The City of Denver's application requires the following:

- Advisement and Acknowledgement Form,

- Affidavit of Corresponding Medical License,

- Affidavit of Lawful Presence for each owner,

- Area map indicating the radius of one-quarter mile around the property to show the proximity away from any school, pre-school or child care establishments,

- Copy of Burglar Alarm Permit,

- Copy of contract with alarm monitoring company,

- Certificate of Good Standing from the Colorado Secretary of State Office, and Articles, partnership or trade name filing,

- City & State Sales Tax License,

- Description of products and services,

- Distance Waiver,

- Floor plan showing the uses of the floor area,

- Government Issued ID for each owner,

- Lease or deed – if property is leased, written consent from the owner of the property

- Security Plan in compliance with security provisions listed in the city's bylaws,

- State License and Zoning Use Permit.

The City of Denver also requires a Community Engagement Plan, which includes:

- Contact information for the person responsible for neighborhood outreach and engagement.

Names of all registered neighborhood organizations in the area and that the applicant contacted them before starting operations.

Outreach Plan to contact and engage local residents and businesses.

Detailed description of any plan to create positive impacts in the neighborhoods (e.g. volunteering, and active promotion of any local neighborhood plans).

Written plan to address any concerns or complaints expressed by residents and businesses.

Written plan to promote and encourage the full participation from communities disproportionately harmed by marijuana prohibition and enforcement.

To read more about the applications process, you can go to Denver's *Retail Marijuana Licenses* website and Washington State's *Marijuana Licensing* website.

Once you are up and running, expect to see the local inspectors come to your dispensary without giving any prior notice. City Inspectors take their jobs seriously. So should you. If they notice any mistakes, correct them in a timely manner. If they suspect criminal activity or the breaking of any of the cannabis laws, they can issue you a fine, temporarily close you for few weeks, or for repeated violations shut you down. It is best to treat them with respect and welcome them into your store. Better yet, think of the City Inspector as a 'must-listen-to' public service advisor. After all, when and if the rules change, having a good working relationship with city officials is a key to your success.

Create a Business Plan

The single most important thing you can do from the start is to write a Business Plan – especially if you need financing. You need a Business Plan that shows the costs and sales, supported by reasonable estimates for potential profits. You can divide your Business Plan into seven parts:

- **Description of the business.** Explain your goals, objectives, and why you want to be in a retail cannabis business. Describe who you are, the hours of operations, type of business, and what products and services you plan to sell.

- **Security Plan.** Security Planning is a critical component of a dispensary's Business Plan. Outline the measures you will take to protect your inventory, cash, building and employees.

- **Marketing plan.** How well you market will determine the degree of success or failure. The key element of a successful marketing plan is to know who your customers are, their likes, dislikes and expectations.

- **Management plan.** Your management plan, along with your marketing and financial plans, sets a foundation for the success of your business. People are a resource. It is vital that you know how to manage and treat your employees.

- **Operations plan.** Cost-controls and inventory management are important parts of running a dispensary. Having good records and a point-of-sale system to keep track of sales and inventory will take a lot of time, but also provides you with good information.

- **Financial plan.** Include start-up costs, any loan applications you filed, equipment and supply costs, balance sheet, break-even analysis, and three-year projected income statement and cash flows.

- **Additional materials:** Includes executive summary, explanations for estimates used in your financial projections and other supporting documents.

Know the Local Laws

Starting a business means following the laws of the land. As soon as possible, find out about the license and permit requirements in your jurisdiction for starting a cannabis business. Each state (provincial) and municipal government will have different regulations. In this book, if you see information about Denver or Vancouver, do not assume the same application requirements will apply to you. Since no one can predict with absolute certainty what your local licensing and permits will include, take the following list below as suggestions of what to expect near you.

Business license. All municipal governments will require a permit to open a cannabis business. Contact your local city centre for licensing information. When applying for your license, be sure your application is 'complete' with all the supporting materials (e.g. tax documents, proof of residency). Oregon requires a $250 non-refundable fee and an initial license fee is $4,750. In Vancouver, this license fee is $5,000 for businesses with cannabis onsite and $500 for those with no cannabis onsite.

City of Victoria's operational requirements:

- No individuals under the age of 19 on the premises.

- No consumption of cannabis on the premises.

- No advertising, other than minimal storefront signage, which can include a maximum of two signs with letters or numbers only.

- Not be open for business between 8 p.m. and 7 a.m.

- Install and maintain an air filtration system to ensure odour impacts on neighboring properties are minimized (for those with cannabis onsite).

- Post health and safety warning signs on the premises.

- Ensure the premises is only for the sale of medical cannabis and accessory uses.

- Only one business license will be issued per location.

- Restrict use of ATMs and vending machines on premise.

- At least two employees must be on duty, one of whom is a manager.

- Windows must not be blocked.

Even if your application is approved, if you do not keep up with the conditions required in the license, you may be closed or fined. In Vancouver, "no less than $250 and not more than $10,000 for each offence." It is in your best interest to comply.

Zoning. With business licenses, you also find the need for zoning permits. Apply for a business license and a rezoning together, as soon as you have all of the required supporting documents. The fee for a cannabis business rezoning application in Victoria, Canada, is $7,500. These permits help cities and towns prevent nuisances from happening in neighborhoods and districts, such as reducing noise, odour, and customer misconduct on and around the licensed business. For instance, Denver requires your dispensary be 1,000 feet from a school.

Building permit. If you plan to renovate your dispensary that makes changes the structural nature of the building, you may need a building permit. Most new businesses will need to make changes at the start. Your local building and zoning board will issue building permits.

Criminal background check. You may be required to submit the names of all staff, together with a copy of their photo identification. Let's face it, your business is attractive to criminal elements. In Nevada, for example, it is required to criminal check on all prospective employees. Those with criminal records are not hired. To obtain a *Criminal Record and Vulnerable Sector* in Canada, prospective employees must submit a full set of all 10 fingerprints, which can be done using an electronic scan. Only an authorized fingerprinting service can perform this task, which costs under $100 (including a $25 processing fee) for each criminal record check.

Sales Tax. Each state or province will have their own method of collecting taxes from the sale of cannabis-related products. Contact your local tax authorities for more information. Certain regions and cities may also add an extra sales tax on top of their state or province's sales tax. Toronto mayor John Tory is advocating for some discussion on this topic. This entire issue of sales tax will still need more guidance from the different levels of government.

Health department license. If your jurisdiction allows you to sell edibles, you will need to contact the local Public Health department. It would be to your advantage to cooperate and comply from the very start. States will one day require that the manager – and perhaps the entire staff – go through and passes an approved health and safety program similar to Ontario, Canada's *Smart Serve* run by the Alcohol and Gaming Commission of Ontario. Your municipal or State health departments will remove all your edible products and can shut down your shop to force you to comply with its regulations.

Fire department permit. You may require a permit from your local Fire Department before opening. The Fire Inspector will be interested in checking fire exits, location of extinguishers and the sprinkler systems before you open. Based on the size of your building, the number of exits and local and national fire code, the Fire Inspector will establish a "capacity number" to limit how many people can be in the building at one time. Follow their guidelines strictly, even if this means turning away customers because you reached your capacity.

Sign permit. Many local governments will pass bylaws and restrictions on retail dispensary signs. These bylaws restrict the sign's size, type, and location of the sign to the business. Shopping center managers may also want to restrict where signs are placed. The City of Vancouver, for instance, limits where dispensaries can advertise and promote, limiting signs to where it can "reasonably" avoid being seen or heard by those under 19 years old.

Hire Competent Experts

For many businesses, the road to success involves many stumbles. Knowledgeable business consultants will help guide you towards success if you are struggling to get started. Note that not every consultant is helpful and that you should do your own due diligence to find the right one for you.

Lawyer. You will need a lawyer for legal advice to get started. Your lawyer can help you negotiate the lease. You may come to have problems with customers, vendors, other tenants, your landlord or your employees. You may also have need for a lawyer who specializes in bankruptcy, litigation, taxation, or patent laws. Before hiring, make sure you ask the lawyer what areas he or she specializes in.

Accountant. At a minimum, a knowledgeable accountant should understand what deductions are allowable under the tax laws. Cannabis businesses may be subject to auditing flags due to the nature of the industry. Your accountant may know professionals (usually a tax lawyer) who are knowledgeable about defending businesses subject to audits. Also be sure to meet with your accountant when you are deciding to buy a new point-of-sale system, so together you can identify the pros and cons of the various software.

Bookkeeper. Your accountant will recommend that you hire a bookkeeper. The bookkeeper works the long hours of keeping track of your financial records. Keeping track of taxes, payroll, inventories and mountains of other regulatory requirements is a lot of work for the business owner alone, along with the regular day-to-day staffing, marketing, purchasing and customer relations issues. An accountant will charge you more for his or her precious time than a bookkeeper will. Hiring a bookkeeper for record keeping will save you time and money in the long run.

Security consultant. A cannabis business license requires a signed agreement with a security company. A security consultant will help you with your Security Plan by recommending the locations of where to put video surveillance cameras inside and outside your store and offer advice on your security and fire alarm system. Your security (and accounting) team will advise you on the best controls to safeguard your valuable assets. To contact a security company that deals with cannabis businesses, go to Securifort-Gardex and Tri West Technologies.

Architect and interior designer. In most cases, you will need to renovate. Some cities will require floor plans. If you are constructing a new building, the City Director of Planning will only grant a development permit after notifying the surrounding property owners and residents and have regard to their opinions. An architect or interior designer who knows about the cannabis industry will advise you on the design needs. To contact an interior design firm that deals with cannabis businesses, go to figure3 and Pot Shop Designs.

Review the Startup Costs

In case you are wondering, start-up costs average about $325,000 US[45] but in some cases could go up to $500,000 US.[46] Still focused on that dream? Okay then, make it happen. Where there is a will, there is a way. Consider these startup costs:

- Early investigation costs
- Working capital
- Licenses and permits
- Legal fees
- Building and construction plans
- Renovations
- Locksmith
- Insurance
- Display cases
- POS system
- Inventory: cannabis-related
- Inventory: non-cannabis-related
- Storage containers.
- Product containers
- Commercial refrigerator for edibles
- Pricing board
- Cash register
- Training
- Safe
- Security system
- Signage for building
- HVAC system
- Website design
- Security deposits for the building, including delays in opening
- Rent or leasing costs before opening
- Employee furniture
- Computer equipment

- Business cards
- Advertising and promotions
- Phone systems
- Sound systems
- Lighting
- Pre-opening labour

- Miscellaneous supplies
- Deposits for utilities
- Store furniture (including office)
- Architect and interior design plans
- Employee area (fridge, table, etc.)

Of course, none of this can happen without first finding a location in the zoned areas of your city. The costs will pile up long before you make your first dollar, and even when you start making money.

Prepare for Contingency Costs

Not having an adequate contingency fund is the main reason many businesses fail within the first few months. You will need to over-hire and over-schedule employees before a sales pattern emerges. Expect the first six months of operations to have high expenses. Make sure you have enough cash available for supplies on hand at the start. It is not uncommon for businesses to fail because of unforeseen expenses. Your contingency fund needs to be large enough for at least the first six months' of operating expenses. This could be an additional 20 percent of your startup budget.[47]

Find Sources of Financing

Like any other small business, the amount of funds you have available will limit the opening of your retail dispensary. You need a large amount of money to lease the property, pay licenses and permits, cover your lawyer's fees and stock your shelves. Since you may need financing from lenders or investors, it is all the more important to prepare a Business Plan to show you have a thorough enough understanding of your business.

Personal savings. Unlike other businesses, dispensaries cannot apply for government-backed small business loans. Most people must instead provide all of the capital themselves in cash, either from their own savings or from family, friends and other private investors. About 72 percent of a dispensary's financing will come from your own savings and debt.[48] If anything goes wrong, and you spend your retirement savings and borrowings, you will have nowhere else to turn. Think carefully if this is the route you want to take since a setback can turn into a very expensive Life lesson.

Family and friend. Private sources could include friends and family willing to grant interest-free or low-interest loans. This is the other most common source for start-up money. Family or friends may consider gifting you the money based on your Business Plan. The major drawback is that if the business fails, you could damage your relationships with them.

Private lenders and investors. Have you ever thought about making a business pitch to a group of people with money that you know (e.g. lawyers, dentists, doctors, professional colleagues, college roommate, etc.)? This could be the new and lucrative business opportunity they were looking for. Arm yourself with a Business Plan and a good pitch.

Home equity. If you own a home, you can obtain a home equity loan or a second mortgage. Most financial institutions allow you to borrow as much as 80 percent of your property's value. Keep in mind that if your business fails, the bank has no hesitation with foreclosing on your home. If this is an option for you, then lock in an affordable interest rate and try to spread your repayments as far out as you can.

Venture Capital

The growth of the cannabis industry means millions of investor dollars looking for businesses. This may not be entirely true for retail operations. Investors in this industry are cautious. By some accounts, 30 percent of all businesses fail – and venture capital and angel investors know this too.[49] As at the time of writing this book, only California-based Green Growth Investments advertises funding "commercial business opportunities in retail" on its website.

Banks and Small Business Programs

If you live in Canada, with the legalization allowing these types of businesses, banks and government-funded small business programs will start making loans to cannabis businesses. That said, banks and small business programs at present do not lend to cannabis businesses. They just don't. If they did – and miracles did happen – here is how potential lenders (or investors) will view your request for money:

- Have you invested savings into the business totaling at least 25 to 50 percent of the loan requested? Remember, no one wants to finance 100 percent of your business.

- Have you prepared a Business Plan that shows your understanding of the business?

- Do you have sufficient experience and training to operate a successful business?

- Does the dispensary show sufficient cash flow projections to provide a return?

- Submit a copy of your credit report from a credit-reporting agency.[50]

Perhaps one day soon banks and other financial institutions will recognize the potential profits and offer you the same loan application process like any other business. But for now, do not hold your breath. Your best bet is to fund your business through your own personal savings and investors.

Take Action

A Business Plan will help set your goals and expectations in motion. The following should help you with setting the early foundations of your cannabis business:

- **Research** the local licensing requirements in your jurisdiction and understand the application process.

- **Write** a Business Plan and review the startup costs, and be sure to include a section for your Security Plan.

- **Select** a team of competent consultants and advisors (most importantly, a good lawyer).

- **Review** all the possible sources of financing that are available to you. Use your Business Plan as a resource to prepare for pitches and presentations to deliver to potential investors or lenders.

With a Business Plan in hand, do you know who your customers are and what do they want?

Chapter 3

Your Customers

"I think for most cannabis consumers, the fact that they walked into a store, showed their ID and bought real legal marijuana for the first time in history was a huge deal. That was two years ago, and it was like, 'Wow, this is great.' And since then, [consumers] are getting hungry [for more information]."[51]

MATTHEW HURON, COLORADO DISPENSARY GOOD CHEMISTRY

In what will become a competitive marketplace, retail stores will soon need to learn more about their customers. For many shoppers, a cannabis store is a new type of business. Whether a customer decides to enter at all, or to tell his or her friends and family about you, will depend on how they see "pot" and how they judge those who use it.

Begin to think of cannabis customers as one of three groups: the medical user, the habitual user, and the newcomer. Your job is to educate them about cannabis. 'Customer for life' is the idea that once a customer comes into your shop, they will never be satisfied with your competitors. Give them a reason to return.

Public Awareness

Canada's federal and provincial governments will soon be rolling out their public awareness campaigns. Mothers Against Drunk Driving Canada has already begun airing cannabis impaired driving television ads. [52] Colorado Department of Transportation currently send out public service announcements for impaired driving.

Government-supported public awareness campaigns will be a significant key towards the acceptance of cannabis. Radio, television, newspaper and social media ads will all help to inform targeted groups, informing young adults, youth, parents, pregnant women, and everyone about the health impacts.

Ontario's Health Minister Eric Hoskins, a physician himself, said, "One of the things that [Colorado' Department of Public Health & Environment] pointed out is that they wish, in retrospect, they had moved on the public education significantly before it became legal. They didn't and so I'm taking that principle to heart. We can't wait until July 1."[53]

While legalization is happening, cannabis still has a stigma. Many people – including longtime cannabis users – fail to understand the health impacts and think pot is all about getting high. Cannabis will be new for many. New words like "terpene", "cannabinoid", "sativa", "indica", "dabbing", "vaping", "THC", and "CBD" will enter our vocabulary. People will soon discover they can also eat and drink cannabis, not just smoke it. Just as a government awareness campaigns will help people to accept cannabis, dispensaries will also play a role in educating people about what cannabis can do.

Cannabis Consumers

You probably have a few ideas about who your customers will be. You might even live in a university town, for instance. But don't be surprised if you discover that most of your customers are soccer moms and dads who would prefer to use cannabis discreetly and don't want their children or neighbors to know.

The Cannabis Consumers Coalition[54] found that:

- 20 percent of cannabis consumers were from lower-income households.

- 35 percent make between $26,000 and $55,000 per year.

- 27 percent have combined household incomes over $75,000.

- 68 percent were men versus 31 percent for women.

- People who use cannabis came from all walks of life.

The market for cannabis is an older crowd. From 2011 to 2015, cannabis users who were 26 years old and older grew by more than 30 percent, compared to those ages 18 to 25 who climbed only about 4 percent.[55] "The guy ripping bong hits every day is not buying higher-end products", said Vivien Azer, a managing director at Cowen who analyzes the cannabis industry.[56] Expect your typical customer to look more like they could shop at Starbucks or Whole Foods or Apple.

Demographics expert Chuck Underwood recommends looking at cannabis consumers through generational profiles:

- **Millennials,** born between 1982 and 1998 (now aged 18 to 34).

- **Generation X**, born from 1965 to 1981 (now 35 to 51).

- **Baby Boomers**, born from 1946 to 1964 (now 52 to 70).

The Baby Boomers launched us into the Drug Revolution. Gen Xers were born into a time that said, 'Just say no to drugs'. Millennials came of age in a time of legalization for medicinal use. Each will have their own customer service and marketing needs.

Understand Your Medical Customers

The medical marijuana patient is an important category of customer. Medical patients choose marijuana treatments to avoid the high prescription costs and the dangers of opioid addiction. High-CBD strains, which offer little to no psychoactive effects, are preferred by patients treating seizures, anxiety and pain.

Growing evidence is showing newer treatment options for neuropathic pain, multiple sclerosis, and nausea from chemotherapy.[57] Depending on a cannabis strain's cannabinoid profile, different types of relief are achievable, such as from chronic pain relief, anti-inflammation, and anxiety relief. Marijuana could also help people with Alzheimer's and other forms of dementia, as well as Parkinson's disease.[58]

HelloMD, provider of online medical consultations, found about 85 percent of medical marijuana users had some form of higher education, with nearly 15 percent having postgraduate degrees. About 45 percent were parents. Younger patients treated anxiety, nausea, insomnia and depression, and preferred smoking or vaping.[59] Older patients treated chronic pains and prefer eating it in edibles or use topicals.[60]

Cody Lindsay is a 32 years old father, certified red seal chef, and a Canadian Forces veteran served in Afghanistan. He and his unit had been unprepared for an unexpected and rapid deployment. After his return, he felt a constant, crippling anxiety. His thought felt foggy and clouded. The sudden deployment, the lack of prep training, leaving his family at a moment's notice, all took its toll.

Veterans Affairs Canada pays for his medical marijuana. He wanted to avoid the mood altering, chemical cocktail of drugs, the pharmaceutical pills that would alter his moods. Cody Lindsay said, "I would not have the ability to be in touch with myself...I enjoy how the CBD-rich strains work so well in edibles and how the CBD helps with a long lasting whole body high, not just a head high".[61]

If you are wondering what CBD is, cannabidiol (also known as CBD) is one of at least 85 cannabinoids found in cannabis, which has a documented medical value for relieving an array of symptoms. Tetrahydrocannabinol (THC) is the other best-known cannabinoid. THC is the main mind-altering psychoactive cannabinoid found in cannabis.

Ruth Brunn is 98 years old and sits in a wheelchair. She has neuropathy, a burning, stabbing, drilling pain in her shoulders, arms and hands. It gets worse in night. Ruth swallows a green pill filled with cannabis oil with her cup of vitamin water and waits for the jabbing to stop. The nursing home in New York City where she lives, the Hebrew Home at Riverdale, helps its residents use medical marijuana as an alternative to prescription drugs. While the staff will not administer cannabis, Ruth can buy it from a dispensary and take it on her own. "I don't feel high or stoned," she said. "All I know is I feel better when I take this."[62]

In addition to capsules, older patients also prefer using topicals. Topicals are cannabis-infused lotions that are absorbed through the skin for relief of pain, reducing soreness and inflammation. Because topicals are non-psychoactive, patients often choose them for therapeutic use without having the cerebral euphoria effects that usually come from ingesting cannabis.

The number of cannabis users 65 and older is small, but their growth over the years as new patients is worth noticing. Some entrepreneurs are looking at older customers as a prime business opportunity. For Ray Taylor, who opened the Healing Center in San Diego, about 60 percent of his customers are age 40 and up. He expected his first customers to come from young stoners, the 20-year-olds looking for a buzz, the Rastafarians. "Seniors and people in that category are going to start using it more and more", Taylor said. "I think there is a huge market."[63]

Meet Your Habitual User Customers

There are no 'typical' cannabis users. Habitual users come from all walks of life. That said, they look a lot like those in the mainstream. A survey of 800 consumers from Miner and Co. Studio found about 84 percent of them worked full-time, 65 percent reported earning a household income of at least $75,000 US per year, and 42 percent had children under the age of 18.[64] The average age for male shoppers is 37.6 years and women are 38.2 years old.[65] Of these retail shoppers, 93 percent of consumed cannabis at least once a week.[66] Following along the same lines, Canada's Parliamentary Budget Office estimates 98 percent of the total demand for cannabis will come from the 41 percent of users who consume "at least once a week".[67] These are your "regulars".

Regular consumers spend a lot of money on cannabis products each year. Lighthouse Consulting, a market research firm based in Toronto, found that "about 21 percent of regular users use cannabis about 2 to 5 times a week, 19 percent every day, and 9 percent once a week. Weekly users smoked an average of 11 grams. About 19 percent spend $100 a month and 21 percent over $200 a month. Premium customers spend over $300 a month on cannabis products. The average cannabis customer in Canada spends $600 a year."[68]

Headset, a cannabis analytics firm based in Seattle, found "most people spend between $25 and $50 a trip to the store, with a $33 median spent per trip. A third of all customers only bought one item, like a pre-rolled joint or a beverage, and spent less than $10. The average customer spent $645 a year and over 57 percent spend more than $500. Less than 10 percent spent more than $2,500." [69]

There is a difference in how men and women shop. The largest percentage of customers is young men. Men make more frequent visits, almost every 19 days, while women go about every 21 days. [70] Here's the catch, while there may be more men shoppers, women buy more. Women buy two items a trip and spend about $35 a trip, compared to men who only spend $33 a trip and put only one or two products in their basket.[71]

Soccer moms (and dads) are common users. Despite legalization happening, there is still a stigma. Most people still want to use cannabis discreetly, not wanting their children or neighbors to know. The pungent odour from smoking can smell up the entire house, so people use it privately.

Cannabis helps soccer moms and dads remain focused, no hangover, and makes mundane tasks like laundry feel easier. This may sound strange to a non-cannabis user to hear that cannabis can help people become more focused and productive. No strain can magically make you more productive, but a balanced strain can "enhance" your outlook towards an activity without losing your concentration.

Here are a few examples of strains – thanks to Leafly suggestions – paired with related activities:

- House cleaning, gardening and grocery shopping: Dirty Girl, Plushberry, Harlequin.

- Going to the gym, hiking: Allen Wrench, Permafrost, Jack Herer.

- Cooking, walking the dog: Buddha's Sister, Dancehall, OG Kush.

- Balancing finances: Pennywise, Brandywine.

For the more affluent soccer mom, MedMen co-founder Adam Bierman has a nickname for what he considers the biggest untapped demographic: "the Chardonnay mom." These customers have the money, who themselves were introduced to it by friends at a party or decided to step into the store while walking by. "They see this store and say, 'Oh, I'll try those breath mints,' " said Bierman.[72] "They start becoming someone who is substituting marijuana for alcohol or something else."[73]

Among habitual users, you also find the connoisseur. They talk about strain flavors (terpenes). The connoisseur is a special type of cannabis customer. Their love of the plant can only be described with the same level of passion and joy as a wine, coffee or gourmet foods lover. With over 100 different terpenes flavors, every strain has a unique in smell, taste and effect. Good cannabis looks good, smells good and feels good to the touch. Bad cannabis does not smoke well. Musty, mildew smells are red flags, and chemical smells a sign of pesticides.

Terpenes are the pungent oils that colour cannabis strains with distinctive flavors, like citrus, berry, mint, and pine that help to medicate the body. Their differences can be subtle. Myrcene, for example, induces sleep whereas limonene elevates mood.

Knowing about terpenes only deepens your appreciation of cannabis whether you're a medical patient or recreational consumer. In a shop, the connoisseur knows he or she cannot touch the flower, otherwise risks contaminating the trichrome. In the light, through a glass jar and a lens, the connoisseur looks for colour and smell.

Higher-income customers can indulge themselves a bit more. Edible Events, a cannabis events company in Colorado, helps host cannabis-infused tastings, food pairings and musical events. They "create a comfortable, indulgent atmosphere to maximize your cannabis experience."[74] THC University in Denver offers gourmet cooking classes.[75] MedMen University offers sommelier training to teach about cannabis-infused tastings and food pairings. The more affluent buy $400 to $3600 cannabis cigars made by Gold Leaf.[76]

Just because people have smoked cannabis for years does not make them an expert. There is another kind of habitual user. After years of it being illegal, a cannabis culture of users has grown without ever knowing much about cannabis. Country singer and longtime cannabis activist Willie Nelson – who even has a strain named after him – does not know much about weed.

In an interview with Wil S. Hylton, New York Magazine, Willie Nelson was asked to compare Sour Diesel and Blue Dream strains. From the story:

"We spent the next hour burning down joints and a collection of vaporizer cartridges filled with marijuana concentrate, but the more we smoked and talked about smoking, the more I began to realize that Nelson knew almost nothing about the plant. He really wasn't sure what kind of weed we were smoking or how the various strains might differ from one another. He had never put a cannabis seed in the ground and didn't intend to. "Why should I grow if this guy over here, or that guy, already has it?" he asked. He also didn't have much interest in the profusion of pot cookies, candies, and soft drinks that have been turning up in the legal states. "I don't like edibles that much," he said with a shrug. "I had a bad experience the first time I did it. This was 50 years ago. I ate a bunch of cookies, and I lay there all night thinking the flesh was falling off my bones." He wasn't even sure about the difference between the two major forms of cannabis, indica and sativa. These are commonly said to have different psychoactive effects, the first being more like a narcotic and the second being more energetic, but when I mentioned these things to Nelson, he just laughed. "I haven't become all that expert on that," he said. "The way I look at it is: I'm either high or I'm not."[77]

Most longtime cannabis users who walk into your shop will be like Willie Nelson. Journalist Hylton continued:

"This discovery frankly thrilled me. Too many pot smokers these days have gotten fussy about their weed. In the same way that modern foodies have eroded the simplicity of homegrown food, leaving behind its rustic roots for a universe of prickly, esoteric greens and incomprehensibly expensive mushrooms, turning local food into a temple for snobs and picky eaters, I have noticed a similar tendency creeping into the conversation around pot — with inflated descriptions of bud density, room-note, fruity undertones, and heritage genetics, usually proffered in the grandiose vocabulary of the dismal jerk who flips out over wine. Nelson was after something simpler. He just liked getting high. He may be one of the most famous stoners on Earth, with a tolerance to fell giants, but he is not, strictly speaking, a marijuana connoisseur."[78]

Learn About the Newcomers

New users will feel the affects of cannabis different than a more experienced user. Cannabis influences everyone differently. Not everyone's first experience will be good. A bad trip can feel like a rush of anxiety, paranoia, dissociation, and a racing heart, causing people to swear off cannabis for life. Some people may not even feel anything the first time. Most will find the experience relaxing and a little euphoric. Some feel more outgoing and social. New users will not be sure how cannabis will affect them. This is where a budtender's informed recommendations on strains and to start with a low dose help.

New users will often ask about the difference between a sativa and an indica strain. Indica strains are known for its physical sedating feeling, perfect for relaxing with a movie or before bedtime, giving a relaxing body high. Sativas provide a more cerebral effects, paired well with physical activity, social gatherings or creative projects, giving an uplifting head high. Hybrids fall somewhere in between this indica-sativa spectrum. A customer suffering from fatigue or depression uses a sativa during the day; while a customer treating pain or insomnia will choose an indica strain at nighttime.

Given the choice in strains and methods to consume, new users won't know where to start. The budtender needs to ask new users three questions: What is your experience level with cannabis? Do you have smoke or dietary restrictions? Where and with who will you be enjoying it with?"

Some tips offered by Leafly for first-time users include:

- Start in a comfortable place. Sometimes being at home is the best place.

- Listen to music you enjoy while trying the strain.

- Laugh to enjoy a moment (e.g. watch a movie, jokes or watch videos).

- Drink water. Hydration can prevent many discomforts caused by cannabis.

- Try a CBD-only product.[79]

If you did not know, CBD counteracts some of THC's anxious side effects. Bailey Rahn of Leafly recommends Harlequin, Sour Tsunami, Pennywise, Harle-Tsu and Cannatonic. For a balanced CBD/THC, recommend Jack Herer, Chernobyl, Plushberry, Maui Waui, and Permafrost.[80]

If customers feel anxiety or paranoia from their first experience, they should:

- Sniff or chew on a few black peppercorns for almost instantaneous relief.

- Go for a walk. This can feel therapeutic for anyone feeling anxiety from cannabis.

- If needed, take hot shower or use aromatherapy to calm anxiety.

Beginners have the choice of starting with smoking, vaporizing or edibles. Newcomers should start with small amounts of flower, especially low doses of edible.[81] Most will begin with smoking, which has the advantage of dose-control. However, vaporizing may be a better option for newcomers. It is easier on the throat and lungs, and the flower's tastes on the tongue adds extra flavor to the experience.

But for some, neither smoking nor vaporizing feels like the healthier option. While edibles avoid the smoking, beginners should start with low doses – maybe just 5-mg – and work up to 10-20-mg.[82] However, if someone is counting calories or has a food allergy to milk, nuts or flour, edibles may not work either. Perhaps topicals? Most topicals will not get you high but will offer a comforting option that soothes the skin. Need to be discreet? Get the breathe mints or an oral spray.[83] And of course, tell new customers to take their time.

Elevate the Language

Cat Piss, Green Crack and Buddy Fucker might not be the names that sell products. Strains and strain names are puzzling for new (and many longtime) customers. Alan Gertner, co-founder of the cannabis lifestyle brand Tokyo Smoke, believes that changing the language around cannabis will play a role in re-defining the customer's experience. "The biggest opportunity for growth is in recreational use and normalization," Gertner said.[84]

Part of escaping the stoner stereotype is using a more refined vocabulary. Alan Gertner advises us to "forget the slang, and speak to a higher conversation. People are beginning to call it 'cannabis' instead of 'pot', 'weed' or 'marijuana'. 'Buds' become 'flowers.' 'Hits' are now 'doses.' 'Bad trip' is called a 'bad experience'."[85]

The trend is towards marketing medical-specific or event-specific branding. Marketing towards specific uses – such as "good for a concert", "good for date night" or "good for Sunday morning" – help to humanize and destigmatize the use of words, presenting products as more intuitive and approachable.[86]

"On the marketing and usability side, we've eliminated the thousands of intimidating strain names like Durban Poison and Train Wreck and have replaced them with our effects – Calm, Cruise, Create, Connect, and Charge," said Adrian Sedlin, CEO of Canndescent.[87] "Instead of Cat Piss and Chernobyl, we offer Calm No. 101, described as 'sedates the mind and body, allowing everything to melt blissfully away' and Create No. 301, described as 'focuses the mind and settles your body, making it ideal for crafts or computer work.' Curating effects and experiences through naming and product descriptions, we hope to put the consumer in control of his or her experience."[88]

Going one step further, Vela, known as the Apple store of pot in Seattle, uses iPads to help customers navigate their list of products based on a customer's mood. Vela created the 'Vela spectrum' to help guide customers. Every product in the store has a designated placard and falls somewhere along the four stages 'Hush, Unwind, Flourish, and Ignite' spectrum. Customers pick up an iPad, pick where they want to be, and the device tells them where to find what applies to them. "Looking at all the product can be kind of overwhelming. This can simplify things," said budtender Joe Craycraft.[89]

Elephant in the Room

Is marijuana addictive? According to psychiatrist John Kelly from Massachusetts General Hospital, "Absolutely, no doubt about it."[90] From a scientific perspective, marijuana abuse does fall within the definition of addiction. Kelly reports this is "similar to alcohol, about eight to 10 percent of the population may be at risk of marijuana addiction, which includes dependence through regular use. Withdrawal symptoms may vary, but include irritability, anxiety, problems sleeping and cravings."[91]

As a problem, however, this observation does not need to feel bleak. When it comes to marijuana, 'one-size' does not fit all. Heavy, frequent, or medical users might consume 50-, 200-, or even 500-mg of THC in one sitting, compared to infrequent users who might get high from 2- or 3-mg of THC. "Compare that to alcohol, people aren't drinking between 2 and 200 cocktails depending on their tolerance", said Eileen Namanny, marketing manager of The Goodship, maker of cannabis-infused cookies, brownies and pastilles.[92] Cannabis is not alcohol. Its therapeutic needs are a big part of its use.

Ross Rebagliati, the first Olympians to come out of the cannabis closet, said, "If you want to call it recreational, go ahead. But to me, it's mental wellness. There's no difference between recreational use and medical use. It's all medicinal. The whole idea that there's a difference between medical and recreational pot is just a bunch of bullshit."[93]

Although regular use over time does increase tolerance levels, users can do proactive things to combat this ebb and flow of tolerance. One recommendation is to rotate strains. Another, to change consumption methods from vaping to edibles. Or change the routine of when you use cannabis, such as not taking it in the mornings. Then again, the best recommendation is to take a "tolerance breaks".

Dante Jordan of Leafly wrote, "Tolerance breaks allow regular users to feel a heighted euphoria, creativity and general wellness after two weeks or more of a break, refreshing the body and mind. With a clear head, customers gain a refreshed respect for the power this plant holds. Customers are reminded that cannabis is an enhancement to life, not a replacement for it."[94]

Take Action

Learning about your customers is critical to the success of your dispensary. The following will prepare you more to understand your customers:

- **Learn** about the difference between sativa and indica strains, CBD and THC cannabinoids, and terpenes. This can be done by reading about the different strains on Leafly. Also learn about what makes a retail cannabis store different from a medical marijuana clinic.

- **Create** customer profiles. Young, old, middle-age, men or women customers, there is no better time to create an 'ideal' customer profile than at the start. You can break cannabis users into three groups: the medical user, the habitual user, and the newcomer. In the beginning, you will start with some assumptions Identify your customers by age, sex, income, education and location.

- **Elevate** the language you use when marketing or describing products for your customers. Uses words more familiar to the mainstream in your advertising to reach more customers.

- **Use** a POS system to listen. When your dispensary is open, use the integrated Customer-Relationship-Management features of your and Point-of-Sales system to send messages and to learn what customers want.

Even though understanding your customers is a critical first step, your next step is to know what makes you different from your competition in your customers' minds.

Chapter 4

What Makes You Different?

(handwritten: L.A. Start)

"What makes this outpost of Have a Heart different from the others in Greenwood and Fremont? A lot, actually. For one, patrons are greeted with an enormous, LED-lit joint sculpture upon entering, as well as a chandelier with a quarter pound of Granddaddy Kush encased in glass. If that's not enough to awe you, there's the 50-foot 'Wall of Weed.' It's something of a flagship project for the mini-empire, and it really encompasses the downtown feel."[95]

BJ JORDAN, HAVE A HEART MARKETING COORDINATOR.

Today's customers are becoming more educated about smoking, vaporizing and eating (and making) edibles – and getting pickier. They want to know more than just how much THC is in a product. They want to know the levels of all the cannabinoids present. They want to know more about the terpenes and the flavonoids like a connoisseur. All of your customers want to know that your products are safe and reliable. In a growing busy market, what sets you apart from your competitors?

Choose the Right Name

Choosing the right name matters. Your name says a lot to the people you want to attract. It tells them something about your focus on and what you sell. Choosing the right business name also has implications on your choices of website domain names and social media profile names.

If you choose a funny or bold name like Buzzed or Puffy Pete's, some would-be customers might never walk into your shop, simply because your name sounds strange. New customers like medical users, seniors with chronic pains, soldiers suffering from PTSD, and soccer moms and dads. To sell cannabis to a mainstream audience, the stereotype of the 'stoner user' needs to end. Choose a name that represents more than just a good time and sounds inviting and appeals to mainstream buyers. Words like "wellness" or "health" might help.

Is your business name also website and social media-friendly? Since most people find dispensaries using the internet and on mobile devices, it makes sense to think of your business name with search engines in mind. To decide which domain names and social media profile names are available, use Namech_k (https://namechk.com). Remember, a small mistake in choosing a name at the start could turn into a legal problem later if someone wants to contest your business name and take your domain name away.

find available names

Because of the demand for attaching "cannabis" and "marijuana" to business names, you might find it difficult to register the name you want. Here are some tips from Godaddy for choosing a domain name, which can also apply to choosing a business name:

- **Make it easy to remember**. Choose a name that is easy to type on search engines. If you tell people your name, you want it to be easy for them to remember and type quickly when on the run. If you use slang ("u" instead of "you") or words with multiple spellings (express vs. xpress), you might be making it harder for customers to remember and to find you.

- **Keep it short.** If your business name is long and complex, you risk customers mistyping or misspelling it. Short and simple is the way to go, if at all possible.

- **Use keywords.** Try using keywords that describe your business and the services you offer. For example, if you are a specialty vape store, you may want to register GreenVapeStore.com. The point is to include keywords that people could use to search for your products or services. This also helps to improve your ranking and traffic on search engines because it makes more sense to your customers when they find you.

- **Target your area.** If your business is local, consider including your city in your name to make it easier for local customers to find and remember.

- **Avoid numbers and hyphens.** In your domain name, numbers and hyphens are often misunderstood. People who hear your website address do not know if you are using a numeral (5) or it is spelled out (five), or they misplace or forget the dash.

- **Be memorable.** There are millions of business names, so having a catchy and memorable name helps. Once you have a name in mind, share it with close friends to ask if it sounds appealing and makes sense. [96]

Know Your Competition

Keeping track of your competitors tells you a lot about what sets you apart. Take your time in studying how your competitors advertise and promote and how they operate their business. Try to think about what their sales strategies might be. Do not be surprised if your competitor next door hires someone with high-end coffee shop, gourmet restaurant or luxury hotel experience to sell marijuana.

To begin, ask questions like:

- Who are your five nearest direct competitors?

- How are their businesses: steady / increasing / decreasing?

- What have you learned from their operations? From their advertising?

- What are their strengths and weaknesses?

- How do their products differ from yours?

If you can, set aside a folder to keep files (e.g. newspaper clippings) on each of your competitors, and update this folder regularly. You need to distinguish yourself from your competition. What does your target market think of you that gives you a competitive advantage?

Points of Difference

To have customers to want to come back and to tell their friends and family about you, you need to find something that makes you memorable and different. Most dispensaries miss the importance of branding and end up delivering a poor customer experience. While not all of the "points of difference" ideas below are appropriate for every shop, they can be a great way to distinguish your shop and for customers to talk about you.

Know Your Customers

Herb House in Seattle learned early on that the two easiest things they could know about their customers was who they are by name and what they liked. Herbs House – you guested it – is in an actual house. Before cannabis was legalized, Herbs House was medicinal-only. In 2015, Herb House became a full-service recreational store. Customers go to Herb House instead other dispensaries for the atmosphere that it brings. Herbs House prides itself as having "a lot of everything." A mural on the high walls just above the cash registers shows a big red dragon getting high. Every three months a new local artist is chosen to showcase their art, after waiting on a waiting list. Customers look through an extensive list of strains in a flipbook neon-green menu. There is a daily special of something that costs $4.20 all day; often it is hard candies or single-gram joints.[97]

unique.

Offer Better Products

Higher Leaf in Seattle won the 2014 Dope Cup award for "People's Choice Best Flower". Higher Life learned early on to offer more than the obvious choice of dried cannabis, but to offer specialty extracts and edibles. This is the best known store in town for its selection of CBD flower, concentrates, topicals, tinctures, and edibles. Medical customers are grateful to find a wide selection convenient, prepackaged goods of teas, body rubs, and marijuana-infused edibles that no other store offers.

Most customers have a hunger to learn more about what products can do for them. Every Friday customers are invited to a workshop where they meet local producers and processors who talk about cannabis products.[98] Higher Leaf also recognizes its medical patients by offering an extra 10 percent discount, along with the usual a 20 percent discount on the every fifth purchase they offer every customer. Higher Life is known for its CBD products. Do you know what do my customers want and are willing to pay? If you want, you could choose to offer other targeted, health-specific products, such as a line of womens' products to help with easing the menstrual cycle.

Find a Good Location

Ruckus in Seattle is tiny dispensary. Not only is it close to main street stores and restaurants, it is known for its range of products and price points, good music, and a warm staff. The walls are filled with paintings, drawings, and collage art. Cannabis products stored in two countertop glass cabinets look like they once held rare butterfly specimens. The space feels almost like a closet. But they have everything you need. Budtender Cole Vreeland calls Ruckus "a small shop" for "local folks".[99] Ruckus found the right place for itself. Most employees live nearby.

Is the shop conveniently located? Are your ideal customers nearby? Can you afford the location? Will your employees live nearby? To find the best place for you, begin by getting a map. Mark the potential locations and draw a six-block radius circle around each of them. Ideally, you will want to walk into a nearby coffee shop and look at the types of customers you might see. Visit the local businesses and ask the owners questions about the area. If you have any local competition, sample their products and look for areas you can do better.

Offer a Customer Experience

Offering a customer shopping experience definitely sets you apart. Herb(n) Elements in Seattle learned a long time ago that customers would measure them on the quality of their staff and presentation. Good customer experience happens when staff knows the products, offer great recommendations, and helps every customer feel as comfortable as possible. Obviously, the opinion of your customers is shaped by the quality of customer service they received.

Herb(n) Elements staff look professional. Although geared toward the recreational customer, the shop always has a certified medical marijuana consultant at the store to answer questions. Depending on the health or connoisseur vibe you want to create, a staff dress code could help you stand out. How about wearing an apron or a white lab coat? This gives the appearance that you know what you are talking about.

Herb(n) Elements also avoids the bouncers, faded windows, and sketchy feeling that customers have when visiting other stores. They chose to locate in a quiet retreat just outside of the city. "We see ourselves as a bellwether of the industry that typifies what recreational retail should be," says Jamie McNatt, assistant manager. "So we want to make our store feel just like any other retail outfit that somebody would walk into."[100]

Take Action

Even in large cities, only so many potential customers will walk in your store – let alone come back. The following should help you think about how you can set yourself apart:

- **Choose** a business name that is memorable and will be used in your website's domain name and available for use on several social media platforms.

- **Study** your competition. Look for what they do and what you will do better.

- **Identify** how your dispensary will know and connect with customers, find a good location, offer better products, and deliver a memorable customer experience.

Always remember that variations of the same things you sell are also available somewhere else. The more you know about what sets you apart, the more you know what products you can offer.

Chapter 5

The Right Product Mix

"Until cannabis is fully mainstreamed – thereby normalizing the use of edibles, capsules, tinctures, topicals, and so on – flower and pre-rolls will likely remain the dominant solo categories. That said, as consumers become more familiar with some of the industry's newer offerings, we can expect to see more multi-product baskets overall." [101]

REPORT BY HEADSET IO, A CANNABIS ANALYTICS FIRM BASED IN SEATTLE, WASHINGTON

A recreational cannabis business is a retail business. Just like any other retail business, the cannabis customer goes into a store with a specific product in mind. In this case, it's to buy 'flower' (marijuana buds). You can call this the "trip driver" product.[102] Even if most customers come into the store to buy one thing, they often leave with more things. Popular impulse buys can come from Auntie Dolores cheese crackers or Dixie Elixir's fudge. No one goes in just to buy cannabis-infused edible, but they end up tossing in other things when they are about to leave.

Connoisseurs and first-timers alike are learning about the CBD/THC mix, terpenes and what makes (say) Blue Cheese different from OG Kush. As they understand their product options, the regular mainstream customer will move our industry away from a stoner customer to a more refined connoisseur one. Customers are discovering they don't need to smoke cannabis, they can vape, dab and transform ordinary meals into cannabis-infused edible feasts. Edibles and vapes are trending in popularity now. Whatever the reason, your job is to keep your customers coming back and have them leave with a smile.

Product Mix

Product mix is what you offer your customers every day (supplemented with seasonal deals and daily specials). While you are creating your Business Plan, take a moment and think about what products you want to sell. Knowing what products to hold will get you started with an early estimate of your inventory costs. Price, profit margin, and choice of popular products will matter to you, but health and safety have to become your top priorities when selling to your customers.

Dried flower. This is your main product. It comes in several different strains. The dried cannabis on display in glass jars, with names like Blue Amnesia and Afghani Kush, will sell for $2.50 to $14 a gram.[103] Most customers will prefer to smoke their cannabis, which is more of traditional way.

Concentrates. Concentrates oils, wax, shatter and tinctures, and are No. 2 in sales, after flower. It is the fastest growing part of the industry. Vape pens, sold as kits with a replaceable oil-filled cartridge, are driving this growth, accounting for 31 percent of all concentrate sales.[104]

Edibles. You can buy chips, cakes, candies and a long list of other edible foods. Chocolate chip cookies, candy, and ice tea powder will sell for $4 to $20.[105] In Colorado, the quick rise of edibles took state regulators and business by surprise when cannabis became legal in 2014 – named a "top foodie trend" in 2015.[106] Tourists were more inclined to buy edibles over flower because they could relate to them as non-smokers, hide and transport them easier.

Glass pipes, bongs, grinders, rolling papers, vaporizers. With the coming of concentrates, you find pipes, dabbers, and hand held vaporizers. These non-cannabis products offer an excellent source of supplemental sales.

Ointments and capsules. Cannabis manufacturers are producing extracts in capsules. Ointments and capsules give people another option because they do not want to smoke. Each capsule gives a different effect, such as one for sleeping and one for energy.

Topicals. Salves, massage oil, lotions, and bath salts are effective for muscle relief, known for soothing and cleansing. On warmer days, consumers buy more topicals, mostly as sun-protective lotions and salves. Since the topical category is one of the smallest, even a small increase in sales activity appears as a significant spike.

Beverages. Beverages are the top impulse buy. Sodas and flavoured drinks are popular. Beverages are rarely single purchases. About 70 percent of the time beverages are included in a basket full of other cannabis-related items.[107]

Clones or seeds. People buy seeds and clones. Clones are parts taken from a cannabis plant that can be remade many, many times from its offshoots. This is also great way to sell plant-growing accessories like pots, soils and growing nutrients.

Other products. Customers want t-shirts, books, glass cleaners, and a whole host of goods.

Empower Your Budtender

The role of a budtender is to provide advice during a purchase. Budtenders listen to the customer describe what he or she is looking to buy, whether it is a medical or recreational product, and then make a recommendation. When the customer ends up buying more than the one item they came in for, that is a good old-fashioned retail 'upsell'.

"Budtenders hold the keys to the kingdom for both brand success and consumer safety and satisfaction. When we have an opportunity to train budtenders on Botanica's products and process we see an upward shift in the sell-through of our products at that particular store," said Lena Davidson, Market Relations at Botanica Seattle, a Washington state edibles company. [108]

Know About Cannabis Safety

While no one has ever died from cannabis overconsumption, ingesting too much can feel unpleasant, anxiety-inducing, paranoia, heart racing, and nauseous. The standard dose or serving of cannabis in Colorado is 10-mg of THC. The edibles experience differs from the smoking experience. When you smoke cannabis, you notice its affects quicker in your system. It takes longer to digest the THC with edibles, so the desired effect is gradual and mellow. When it's slower, you notice it less, even though the change may still be occurring. The amount of time it takes for an edible to take affect will depend on a person's metabolism. Some people with faster metabolisms may start to feel the effects after about an hour, while those with slower metabolisms may not feel anything for two hours or more.

Metabolizing cannabis makes the effects much stronger. An important factor is whether you consumed the edible on an empty stomach or after you have already eaten. An empty stomach will feel the effects much faster, while a full stomach will not hit you as hard. To avoid feeling uncomfortable, take Lindsay of Dixie Elixirs's advice: "Eat a meal, and then try an edible. Food does not have the same effect for edibles as it does for alcohol. If you feel like you have taken too much, eating a meal can actually push more into your system rather than dilute what's already there."[109]

The effects peak up to four hours after eating or drinking cannabis, so it is best to wait at least that long before consuming more. If you have a new user who has a low tolerance, offer a lower dose of 1 to 5-mg THC amount edibles and products.

Although regulators have called public health and safety a top priority, cannabis-infused products remain largely unregulated. Any food, regardless of whether it contains cannabis, poses public health risks if poorly prepared, mislabeled or made with unsafe ingredients. As such, some degree of regulation is inevitable.

Even if regulators are not ready to allow edibles sales once legalization starts, recreational cannabis users will still be able to cook or bake their own edibles — just like legal medical marijuana patients can do now.[110]

Concerns on safety include:

- Need to maintain THC and CBD levels for medicinal effects and benefits

- Need to exclude harmful levels of pesticide from cannabis production and processes

- Proper dosage shown on labeling

- Child safety

After legalization in Colorado, New York Times columnist Maureen Dowd ate an amount of THC-laced candy intended for 16 people due to a misunderstanding. She didn't feel the effects immediately, so she ate more. "I strained to remember where I was or even what I was wearing, touching my green corduroy jeans and staring at the exposed-brick wall," she wrote. "As my paranoia deepened, I became convinced that I had died and no one was telling me. It took all night before it began to wear off, distressingly slowly."[111]

There has been a spike in visits to veterinarians to treat stoned dogs and cats. Most labeling explains the correct amount to consume and warning about keeping edibles away from pets and kids. But these types of accidents do happen. Admissions to children's hospitals in Colorado for cannabis-related reasons almost doubled after legalization, with about half the cases involving edibles.[112] New rules in Colorado now require standardized symbols (! THC) on edibles, along with banning the word "candy" or "candies" on packaging, as well as banned candy edibles "in the shape of an animal, fruit or character".[113]

A delay in feeling intoxicated before driving can lead to impaired driving, warns Robert Mann of the Centre for Addiction and Mental Health in Toronto. "You can consume a much larger dose than what you might get when you smoke. That creates all kinds of concerns about what the impact will be on driving."[114]

Dabbing is a newer experience in the cannabis world. Dabs are concentrated doses of cannabis made by extracting THC and other cannabinoids using a solvent like butane or carbon dioxide, resulting in sticky oils commonly referred to as wax, shatter, budder, and butane hash oil. The biggest positive is that it gives a powerful dose of medicine. Patients dealing with chronic pain or extreme nausea report immediate and effective relief.

Glass bongs and substances heated with blowtorches have led to the comparison that dabs are the "crack" of pot. The process of extraction can be dangerous – explosive – if done by ignorant DIYers. Another side effect of poor extraction is "dirty" oil that may contain chemical contaminants. One of the most unsettling facts about dabs is that for the first time it seems possible to "overdose" on cannabis. While not lethal, it can feel uncomfortable and cause some people to pass out.

Yes, the dangers are real, but they can be controlled in a professional environment. While dabbing may be going through its awkward phase of public acceptance and use, concentrates have much to offer patients and consumers and is just one more option among others.

Train Staff Like Smart Serve

Every cannabis shop employee is responsible for preparing and serving safe, quality cannabis products. There is no better investment than in training your staff to know about product safety. Ontario, Canada, offers an alcohol server training program that is approved by the *Alcohol and Gaming Commission of Ontario* for servers in the hospitality industry. There are calls to create a similar training and certifying program for those who serve cannabis. Employees must be familiar with basic safety and sanitation practices to reduce the spread of contamination. You must provide employees with the training, knowledge and tools that will enable them to establish and practice proper product handling.

Customer Education is the Key to Safety

"Mg" measures of potency are not well understood. Colorado, for example, declared that 10-mg makes a single serving. People do not know what 10-mg means. Nor do they understand that edibles take longer than smoking to take effect. Because it takes 30-minutes to two hours for a person to feel the effects, people have continued to eat more to feel something. Thus, for a retail dispensary, proactive education take the form of brochures, literature, and infographics, as well as precautions on product labels. The knowledgeable budtender is there to offer advice to both the advanced and novice customer.

Suppliers Must Comply with Standards

Your suppliers and vendors will need to comply with laws and regulations.

Recognize Product Safety Packaging and Labeling

Under many cannabis laws, retail businesses are required to sell cannabis that has been packaged and labelled in accordance with the regulations. In particular, retailers must comply with packaging and labeling laws that require:

- No packaging or labeling that appeal to people under the age of 21 (18 or 19 in Canada);

- No testimonials or endorsements displayed;

- No depiction of a person, character or animal, whether real or fictional;

- No association of cannabis or brand elements that evokes a positive or negative emotion about of a way of life, such as glamour, recreation, excitement, vitality, risk or daring; and

- No information that is false, misleading or deceptive or that is likely to create an erroneous impression about the characteristics, value, quantity, composition, strength, concentration, potency, purity, quality, merit, safety, health effects or health risks of the cannabis.

Suppliers Must Use HACCP

The goal of purchasing is to obtain consistently safe, quality products that meet your menu requirements. Although product safety is primarily the responsibility of your suppliers, it is your job to choose your vendors carefully. Your suppliers are required to meet health and safety standards, and to place their products in leak-proof, tamper-proof, and durable packaging.

Hazard Analysis and Critical Control Points (HACCP) is a six-step program designed for food safety, but cannabis manufacturers can use it to prevent cross-contamination. As governments develop regulations, cannabis cultivators, extractors and infused product manufacturers should look to HACCP for guidance for improving their quality controls.

Let vendors know upfront what you expect from them. Before doing business with them, ask to see their most recent board of health sanitation reports. Put product-safety standards in your purchased specification agreements.

Establish Receiving Procedures (LA)

The goal of receiving products is to obtain fresh and safe cannabis products, and have them transferred to storage areas as soon as possible. Never allow visitors to come into the back areas unless scheduled by the manager. No exceptions!

Schedule all emergency visits by vendors (e.g. repairs to heating or air conditioning), where possible. The only people who will enter without prior notification are government officials, the police, fire department or other first responders for an emergency.

When deliveries arrive, make sure your receiving area is equipped with carts for transporting goods. Managers should check the labels for dates and reference information. Reject all opened or damaged packages. Let vendors know you will be inspecting trucks on a quarterly basis.

−End

Take Action

Your goal is to delight your customers, to win their loyalty and to keep them coming back. The following should help with some ideas on how to set up your product mix:

- **Commit** to establishing delivery and product standard from vendors. Have receiving and HACCP standards written into your purchase agreements. Inform staff, vendors and customers about the importance of safety as a priority, especially for edible safety.

- **Train** staff to know the right words to say to customers when it comes to product safety. Recognize the value of a knowledgeable budtender brings to customers.

Now that you have a better idea of the products available to you, it is time to think of setting up a profitable menu.

Chapter 6

Menu Planning

"There is music setting a tone. There is terpene (plant) extracts in my centerpieces that are creating an aroma. There is art everywhere that is creating and stimulating conversation. So now it becomes an immersive experience where you are present in the dining experience."[115]

CHRIS SAYEGH, THE HERBAL CHEF, COMBINES FOOD AND CANNABIS

Barry Schwartz published *The Paradox of Choice: Why More is Less.* Looking at McDonald's restaurant as an example, Schwartz found that offering too many choices led to customers feeling dissatisfied. "There are three things that having too much choice does," Schwartz explains. "One, it paralyzes people into not choosing. Second, it induces people to make worse choices. Third, even when you make a good decision, you are less satisfied with it. Because as you are munching your Big Mac, you are thinking of all the attractive options you said 'no' to. And the result is that Big Mac doesn't taste as good."[116]

There are no hard and fast rules for knowing how many strains to stock up on, but in much the same way as Schwartz's findings, <u>you want to be careful not to overwhelm your customers.</u> Estimate 60 to 75 percent of items sold on your menu will come from 11 to 15 strains regardless of how many choices you offer.[117] It's still a good idea to offer at least between 25 to 30 strains, along with a new variety "special" each week.

Remember, this applies only to flowers. You also need to consider how many topicals, edibles, concentrates and vape brands to include, let alone include books, rolling paper, and other accessories into your selling product mix. In these cases, you will want to offer less choices than you would for strains; and offering well-known as well as local brand names could be a good start. But knowing your customers and the trends in the market will help to shape what you will offer.

Profitable Menu Planning

Every dispensary has a style, theme, and atmosphere that are important to match to your menu. Try to match your menu choices to the feel of your dispensary. As you learn more about what your customers want, your menu selection will depend on what is available, costs, and the selling prices.

Start with Your Location

The first and most important step for your menu plan is to think about your location. Are you downtown in a chic-location or is it near a main street mall complex? What are people looking for in your area? Is there a local fish market store or bakery? What is currently popular and what are the niche and specialty products you could be known for? What are the socioeconomic considerations in my area? Some areas could offer opulence without alienating customers. You want to offer something different and interesting that attracts customers from all walks of life.

Focus on a Specialty

Most shops will want to offer a diverse variety of products in each category (e.g. dried flower, edible products, beverages, etc.); however, we recommend that by concentrating on a specialty product or two (e.g. edibles and concentrates), and tying together family basket cannabis product "themes" (e.g. moods, health-specific, or event), you will develop a stronger reputation for serving a consistent, quality product and presentation.

A fine-tuned, tailored menu will also help your staff to become more experienced and skilled with each item. They can concentrate on promoting and recommending things your shop does best. By combining complementing product families in different ways – such as cannabis-infused, sandalwood-scented bath salts, topicals, and low dose edible packages – you offer more choices but still have control over your inventory costs. Purchasing that centers around a few major products allows customers to see price breaks and above-average services for larger buys. Menus with more options certainly have a broader appeal, but by keeping products simple, it is easier to provide a quality product and for your staff know your products well.

simple but w/ variety of choices

Create Menu Categories

Start by listing categories of indica-dominant, sativa-dominant, and hybrid introductory strains on your menu. In selecting strains, you can find a list of strains by typing words like "list of" "top", "trending", "best", "medical", "popular", "cannabis strains" in a search engine. Leafly.com also has an excellent directory of strains.

You can also ask your potential customers for feedback in surveys. When business is moving you can use your POS system to keep track of best-sellers and new strain recommendations to discuss any new orders with your suppliers.

use POS & other software to track what sells best & other trends

Focus on Your Customers

Consider offering only products compatible with your store's vibe and anticipated customers. For example, if you have a medical or health therapeutic focus, plan your menu around those particular areas that you want customers to identify with you. Try to include items not easily available in other stores. Ideally, your dispensary should move towards serving only those menu items that you can offer better than any other store.

LA end

Buy Local and Organic

Each region has its own unique flavor. The local and organic movement is also alive in the cannabis world. People love to know their cannabis was locally or organically grown. Local means farmed nearby, a reduced environmental cost and encouraging local economy. Organic means growing without pesticides or plant growth chemicals.

Craft producers, like local wine producers, can offer a local flavor for buyers who want to know where their products came from. Some examples local bred strains in Canada include:

1. **Blue God** (indica), bred by Jordan of the Islands in Canada, has a berry aroma and may help with pain and sleep disorders.

2. **Blue Dynamite** (indica), bred by Next Generation Seeds in Canada, provides heavy mind-and-body relaxation alongside a fruity, hashy flavor.

3. **Chemo** (indica) or UBC Chemo, British Columbia, offers a subtle woody aroma and potent medicinal effects perfect for patients treating nausea, appetite loss, pain, and sleeplessness.

4. **God Bud** (indica) can give users an almost hallucinogenic high while tasting of tropical fruit with undertones of berry, lavender and pine.

5. **Island Sweet Skunk** (sativa), grapefruit aroma, users enjoy for its energetic effects, invigorates the user while still offering anti-inflammatory and analgesic effects.

6. **Lethal Purple** (indica), bred by Great White North Seeds in Canada, has a floral aroma, and offers full-body relief with mental clarity.

7. **Lowryder** (hybrid) can survive in harsh, colder climates, making it a popular strain in northern regions like Finland and Canada. Pungent lemon aroma, creative, energetic effects, helps with nausea and sleeplessness.

8. **M-39** (indica), wood, earthy and lemon aroma, good for relaxation and sleep.

9. **Manitoba Poison** (hybrid), Manitoba, earthy, cheese aroma, delivering deep relaxation that easily converts to a good night's sleep.

10. **Romulan** (indica), pine-scented found in British Columbia and the Pacific Northwest. A deep, sedating

relaxation, a favorite for treating muscle spasms and nerve damage.

11. **Sweet Tooth** (indica), bred by Jordan of the Islands in Canada, has a berry, flowery aroma, providing uplifted and euphoric effects that are great for combating stress and headaches.

Menu Niche

"Niche" is defined as a situation or activity especially suited to a person's interests, abilities, or nature, especially in an area of demand for a product or service. When it comes to cannabis trends, the budtenders is the expert who has to be aware of what customers want or might be interested in learning. Safety, taste, health, and convenience are four key areas that most cannabis consumers want that you can use to market your products.

Focus on Safety

Some customers have a concern about allergens when it comes to edibles. Nuts, soya, milk and flour are the most common intolerances and allergen in edibles. Some customers want to know the exact details about the potency, genetic information, and more before buying. Most people will want only chemical-free and organically-grown products, compared to street bought cannabis that can have harmful pesticides or molds that is more toxic when burned and inhaled. This is why people will prefer legally grown cannabis, where regulators established standards for delivering quality, free of chemicals and mold. This is also why most shoppers are willing to pay extra – for peace of mind.

Offer Tasty Indulgences

Some customers will want to find rich terpene smells and tastes, and edibles laden with expensive ingredients. The potential for developing a culinary market for oils and butters is a growing.

Sell to the Health-Conscious

Some customers want antioxidant-rich flavonoids, natural ingredients, and advice on what will help in preventing diseases or discomforts. Healthy product choices come with scientific evidence – and sometimes the latest fad (e.g. how cannabis can help you to have better sex). Budtenders can talk about the health-related trends when describing the choices of products.

Prepare for Convenience Shoppers

People come in to buy one thing, but then impulse buying takes over and ends up throwing more products into the basket. Vape pens and concentrates are "trip drivers" for most single basket purchase. Some customers only know what they want only when they see it. Preparing convenient, prepackaged goods makes it easier for customers to shop. Small, sellable serving sizes are easy to package. Busy lives mean less time preparing things, so why not prepare ready-made joints for sale?

Menu Specialization

You might think of the idea of "niches" and "specialization" as narrowing down your plan of selling to as many people as possible. But as marijuana moves into the mainstream, dispensaries will be using social media and email marketing to create stronger customer loyalty in a finite and saturated market. It is going to get hypercompetitive. The days of high profit

what sets you apart => specialization

margins will come to an end. In a sea where every dispensary looks the same, you have to think about what will set you apart. This is where specialization comes in.

Leslie Jordan Clary, owner of Leafy Botanical, suggests a retail cannabis store can focus on serving the following niche offerings:

- **High-end concentrates:** potent hash for "dabs" with a high price tag.

- **Vegan/organic cannabis:** marijuana chemical-free and specialize growing methods.

- **Discounted bulk purchases:** selling bulk amounts (e.g. 30-grams) at lower prices.

- **Wide variety of edibles:** appealing to non-smokers who prefer to eat cannabis.[118]

Unlike "niches" that focus on products, "specialization" is your opportunity to establish yourself as an industry expert and the go-to store. For example, if you prefer edibles as your niche, you can set up cooking courses. If you sell wellness products, you could offer complementary spa services. It is important to think about who your customers are and what they want, and from that to know what you can deliver better than anywhere else.

establish a specialization niche to attract patients

Collaborate with Staff and Suppliers

Once you finalize the menu, you and your staff will need to become thoroughly familiar with every aspect of each product. Take your time to find out everything you can about the product.

Ask your staff:

- Which products do they use themselves?

- Which products would they recommend to friends and family?

You also want to talk to the manufacturers and cultivators to assist you in choosing products. Ask them about:

- Where did the ingredients come from?

- Which is the best type or brand?

Do as much research as you can into the newest and most popular strains and products. You will want to stand out from all the other businesses and be the first one to offer the most current products. Listen to your customers, too, and find out what they would like to see offered.

Plan the Menu Prices

Setting up your prices is an important step in marketing. This decision has a direct effect on your bottom line: profit. Canada's Parliamentary Budget Office estimated the pre-tax selling price of legal cannabis would not go below $6.67 a gram, with a midpoint estimate around $7.50.[119] "There will probably be some stuff which is five bucks, (but) I suspect that you're going to find an average price of $7 to $8 a gram," said Bruce Linton of Canopy Growth.[120] This is as low as we expect prices to go. However, prices can go higher.

Consumers tend to think of a higher price as a signal for better quality, status or a product's reputation. People are willing to pay more if they see that extra cost as adding extra value. Cannabis producer Canndescent, for example, sells jarred flowers in humidity-packed, child-resistant glass to preserve the crystalline structures and freshness. They place strains in Chanel-like packaging with a welcome letter in each box. To ensure their strains are always of a high and consistent quality, they use six sigma quality control techniques.

"No doubt, it is thousands of branding and operating decisions like these that have earned us a price premium of 25 percent above most other top-shelf flower in California,'" said Adrian Sedlin, CEO at Canndescent.[121]

With this in mind, how you set your pricing is essential to the success of your business. Set prices high enough to achieve a reasonable profit margin, yet low enough to keep your merchandise affordable and competitive.

[Handwritten margin notes: "portray extra costs as added value x quality"]

[Handwritten notes at bottom: "Compostable pop top tubes are 50¢ more but we can charge $2 more b/c its compostable." "People will pay more b/c its GREEN"]

Know the Costs Associated with Products

First, know the costs associated with your product. Two key elements of costs to include when calculating product price: cost of goods and operating expense. The cost of goods includes the amount paid for the product, plus any shipping or handling expenses. The cost of operating the business, or operating expense, includes overhead (rent, utilities, insurance), payroll, marketing, and office supplies.

Use a 50 Percent Markup Rule

50% mark-up rule

Jeff Grissler, author of *Marijuana Business*, recommends that even though there is no hard and fast rule for pricing, most retailers use a 50 percent markup.[122] What this means is doubling your cost to establish a retail price For example, if your cost on an item is $1, your selling price will be $2. Fifty percent of $2 is $1, which is your markup. This guesstimate is strictly for buying merchandise from a manufacturer, cultivator, or distributer.

Check Your Competitors' Prices

An important part of determining your business's potential is to study the competition. Examine what they offer and what they don't. Look for weak spots in their quality, presentation and selection. Managers will also need to research what the market is willing to pay. Remember to strike a balance with pricing. Your shop could be well-known by cannabis connoisseurs and its knowledgeable staff, but if your prices are too high for your area and target market, customers will stay away. If too low, then you lose profits and maybe some reputation for the quality.

Start Flexible and Change Often

Your first menu should not be your last. You need to be able to remove things that don't work and for new things to see if they could be more successful. Regularly changing your menu is not only a great way to find out what works but also a way to build excitement for your customers around seasonal events. Try to find a regular schedule for change and stick to it. Remember to revisit your menu for changes at least once a year.

be adaptable!

Take Action

From the start, one of the toughest things to do is to create a menu. The next hardest is to change it. The menu is what will bring in customers. Pleasing them with the right menu is important. When it comes to selecting the product mix, remember you are keeping the best mix and changing the rest.

- **Research** cannabis consumer trends to understand how product safety, health, indulgence, and convenient packaging are affecting customers' choices.

- **Research** the flower strains and different products available to stock your dispensary with. In most cases, your choice of suppliers will depend on your location, the nearest suppliers, and your local customers' preferences.

- **Create** a limited menu with the help of your staff and vendors. Think about how you can selling niche and specialty products no other store offers.

KEY ⇒ get in GOOD with sales reps + vendors

- **Set** product prices based on a combination of overhead costs, competitor prices, and markup you need to make a profit.

Now that you know about the products, it is time to think about how your location and interior design will attract customers.

L.A.
end

Chapter 7
Location and Building Layout

"Prospective cannabis entrepreneurs truly need to embrace a changing and challenging startup environment. Even those with significant experience or capital will experience the growing pains and steep educational curve that all new entrants to the industry are met with. They must also be excited by the prospect of social good being a prerequisite for financial success, as the established leaders of the cannabis industry hold these values increasingly important."[123]

MICHAEL BOLOGNA, CEO OF GREEN LION PARTNERS, A DENVER-BASED BUSINESS STRATEGY FIRM FOCUSED ON EARLY STAGE DEVELOPMENT IN THE CANNABIS INDUSTRY

Your location says a lot about you, your brand and the customers you want to attract. Your first problem at the start will be to find the right place. Securing the perfect location can prove nearly impossible for most first owners.

Some towns and cities will restrict where you can open. Some locations might be saturated with existing cannabis stores, forcing you to look farther outside of your local area. Landlords could reject your proposal outright or never return your calls. Some people just want nothing to do drugs. Local councils may even start passing new restrictive bylaws, such as being at least 1,000 meters from other dispensaries in addition to schools. Worse yet, reluctant local government could put up roadblocks to stall legalization in your area. Local taxes could also hinder your choice of location. Even if you find a place, you might not like it. The streets and sidewalks near the business could be in need major repairs. Is location right for attracting your target audience? Is the interior design right for your audience?

Good Neighbor Policy

So much of what we know may happen with legalization is speculative. It is difficult to predict how dispensaries will fit into existing neighborhood planning. But we do know what has happened in Colorado and Washington, where recreational sale has been regulated for years.

Journalist Chad Finkelstein of the National Post found that "restaurant alcohol sales went down between 2 to 4 percent in Colorado. In Washington, the gap between alcohol and cannabis sales has been closing, $212 million for cannabis and $249 million for alcohol. In 2016, the biggest beer brands saw sales 2.4 to 4.4 percent down in states that legalized. People are deciding between cannabis and alcohol. When it comes to food, restaurants found no difference in food sales. So no, cannabis sales did not lead to increased food sales. In fact, restaurants are wondering whether they can cook with cannabis or sell prepackaged edibles. One problem for restaurants, however, is they are losing workers to cannabis retailers and producers in Colorado. In many cases, employees can earn $20 to $22 per hour with full benefits, which is a big lure for workers."[124]

Businesses around the dispensary may start to worry about the need for extra security. Close to a third of crime in Denver have occurred within 1,000 feet of a dispensary.[125] About 7,000 crimes happened near dispensaries in 2013, up 1.8 percent from the previous year.[126] Journalist Chad Finkelstein wrote that "although there is a clear connection between increased crime and marijuana following legalization, it made up less than one per cent of the overall crime in Denver. Most cannabis-related crime is connected to store break-ins – violent crimes are very rare."[127] But the idea of having a cannabis store nearby might raise red flags for neighboring businesses.

There is also an impact on walking traffic (in particular, for families) since some customers may not want their children near patrons who could decide to consume nearby. Even though the laws make it illegal to consume cannabis near or on the premises, some customers and medical users might do so anyway.

If you are located in a shopping center and share a common wall with another shop, make sure you have a good ventilation system. If not, the store next door will smell like marijuana and people will complain. Keep in mind that healthy air inside and outside with proper ventilation is often one of the legal requirements of having a business license. *air quality*

It is always a good idea to have a 'good neighbor policy'. Neighboring businesses can make your life a living hell. Before choosing a location, you might want to ask surrounding businesses if they approve of having dispensary near them, so you don't have to move out later because of a complaint to the city. It would also be helpful if your local Chamber of Commerce supported the opening up of new businesses like your retail cannabis store.

Choose a Location *L.A. Start*

Once you know where the city or town has zoned for cannabis businesses, start to think about where you will to find the best locations. Cannabis-zoned retail areas can become as pricey as waterfront properties, so you need to do your homework. Questions to ask while choosing a location:

Does the area attract the customers you want? If you are interested in a particular neighborhood, talk to the local coffee shop and restaurant owners. How are their customers dressed? What do customers buy from the stores and when do they shop? Can customers see your location at night? Is this a safe neighborhood? Will the businesses around you help to attract customers? Small retail dispensaries can benefit from the traffic of larger nearby stores. Is the parking and public transit adequate? In general, the more the foot traffic, the less the cost for advertising. However, do not confuse high traffic areas with having better walk-in customers. You want a location only if your customers are willing to come to your location.

Is the location conveniently located? The recreational retail business requires you to be there every day. When you choose a location, think about how far the business is from home. If you need to drive your kids to school, how far is it from the shop? A long drive will lessen your enthusiasm for work if you end up traveling too much. In case of trouble, are the police and fire station nearby? Will you find qualified employees in the area?

Are competitors nearby? When choosing your location, look at how many dispensaries are there. Ideally, you want to be the first dispensary near a popular centre that draws people to the area (e.g. a busy coffee shop, downtown location).

Is the building in compliance? Is the space large enough? Quantum9, a Chicago cannabis consulting company, recommends a size of at least 2,500 to 3,500 square feet within the dispensary.[128] In addition to other compliance measures, the Disabilities Act in your local area may require wheelchair ramps and an automated entry button for the entrance door.

Are there other costs involved? Consider the amount of other monthly costs to your budget, such as lawn care, building maintenance costs and property taxes.

Negotiate the Lease

Most dispensaries will operate in a leased building. For the few that own the land the business rests on, the real estate property will often become your most valuable asset. Realize that your rent will be one of your biggest monthly costs.

Taking your time to negotiate your lease agreement at the beginning will save you money. Any miscalculations will be with you the entire term of the lease. Take the lease to a lawyer who specializes in lease agreements. Your lawyer will raise any red flags and explain exactly what you are about to sign. He or she will advise you on how to set up a 'buyout' termination clause, which will allow you to leave the lease if the City Inspector rejects your initial application. Your lawyer may even be able to lock in your rent rate from increasing over the next 10 years, and get you the option to buy at the end. Keep in mind the laws could change, causing you to no longer be in compliance. A smart, knowledgeable lawyer is what you need.

Make a Good First Impression

For years, bong shops have had the grungy look of tinted windows, heavy security doors and flickering fluorescent lights. It looked ugly. The dispensary's customer experience will need to change to reach the wider mainstream.

"I'm more inclined to go to a store that looks better," said Ron Friedman, a retail expert at Marcum in Los Angeles.[129] "It's more than just going in to buy a product, it's creating an environment where somebody enjoys just being in the store."[130] "It's a legal product — this is how it should be," said Ira Levine, a 64-year-old editor and writer, who spends about $400 every two weeks at MedMen to help relieve symptoms from a nerve condition." [131]

An attractive "front entrance" is a powerful invitation for people to come in. Well-planned exteriors invite passersby to stop and come inside. Set your dispensary apart from the bland, industrial looking leased spaces in malls and office buildings with flower awnings, murals and flower boxes. Other ideas that can help to leave a good first impression include:

- Post menus and "daily special" outdoor signs to lure in potential customers passing by. (Restrictions may apply in your local area.)

- Add the right artwork to your shop, which may mean hiring an artist.

- Play music to set the mood, heard through exterior speakers. (Again, restrictions may apply, especially if your dispensary is inside a strip mall).

Journalist Shan Li of the Los Angeles Times wrote that dispensaries "need to embrace a strategy familiar to anyone who has ever spent $5 for a cup of coffee: people like to spend more at a store with upscale ambience."[132] When it comes to finding a unique look, feel, or vibe for your dispensary, you have to think about what would be a fit for your customers.

Setup Public Areas

focal point ⇓ mural

Part of your store's appeal is what it looks like inside. How you decide to design the inside your shop will accentuate your products. Create a focal point that helps define what sets you apart. Think about how you want to show your merchandise and your work areas (e.g. display counter). For instance, is the shop designed for Baby Boomers or Millennials? If you are targeting

Baby Boomers, then they might appreciate the Grateful Dead décor.[133] If you operate in a trendy urban area where mostly mid-forty-something, professionals work, they might appreciate a more contemporary, modern, high-end style, and the 90s rock memorabilia. (The point is, when it comes to interior design, decide what would meet your mainstream audience's tastes. The challenge is to offer many choices without looking cluttered.)

Warmth with Ceilings

consider the ceiling design too!

Without realizing it, ceilings give a room a warm and cozy feeling. Think of your ceiling as another wall to decorate that can add drama to a room. You can have a plain ceiling or an intricate one. If you have a modern interior, your ceiling can show sleek lines or curves. Even a traditional store can show sophisticated moldings.

Brighten with Lights

A well-designed ceiling works well alongside well-designed lighting. Good lighting creates a mood, enhances décor, and makes it easier to sell products. Customers will want to judge a strain's freshness by looking closely at the colors and trichrome before deciding to buy – and good lighting helps with that sale. Invest in proper lighting when designing your retail store.

Show with Counters

Staff present the products at counters. Make sure this is the largest area in your store. You can also leave magazines, brochures or infographic educational materials on countertops for customers to pick up or to read while waiting.

Impress with Your Floor

Although people might not think about flooring as important, it plays a vital role in influencing a customer's overall impression of the shop. In a busy shop with lots of foot traffic, floors with scuffmarks leaves customers with a subconscious feeling that this place is dirty and that products could be of poorer quality. Whenever possible, choose commercial grade flooring that does not show scuffmarks.

Showcase with Displays

Display areas are the best way to show the world what you offer. A great looking display will boost your bottom line by urging more impulse buys. The style you choose to display your merchandise should connect with your customers. Knowing your product mix and store layout will help you decide the best display cases for your needs. Think presentation, presentation, presentation.

Window Display

With some basic carpentry, fabric and creativity, ordinary materials can turn window dressing into a lure for window-watchers to feel welcomed, and enter. Keep in mind that cannabis laws in general restrict certain displays of merchandise or ads that can be seen by those under the minimum age, so make sure your window display meets your jurisdictions requirements.

Display Cases

Display cases will often have shelves. Horizontal display cases can show your choice of specialty glass pipes. Vertical cases to show select manufacturer vape pens from top down. When choosing products to display, think about putting the most expensive products at the top, the high-profit products in the middle (impulse items) and the low profit, bulk and generic brands on the lowest shelves.] *display order logic*

When displaying cannabis flower, look for glass containers instead of plastic bags. Glass is nonporous, giving your cannabis a longer shelf life, and it runs no risk of chemicals leaching from the plastic into your flower (and, by extension, your body).[134]

always go for glass not plastic

Countertop Displays

Eye-level displays on your counter are quite effective in selling new or convenience accessories. These displays can be cardboard displays made by the supplier or glass units that can be seen by customers for easy to pick up, last minute buy.

Selling non-cannabis related products like pipes, dabbers and hand held vaporizers can become excellent profit centers. When selecting displays, think about how to stack rolling papers, display quirky gift ideas and pipe replacement pieces. You can create an area away from the cash register to display them, or place them next to their companion items.

Prepare Backrooms

L.A. start

Backrooms need to be kept secure from intruders and unwanted visitors.

Delivery Areas

Whether your dispensary has a back access door or a loading dock, you need to set up equipment and procedures to accept, log in, and that move goods into storage. Your employees must know these proper acceptance procedures. As a manager, you will need to set up procedures so that you catch ordering and vendor shipment errors.

Accessible Storage

Your storage area should be convenient for deliveries and for employees to access. Manages need to establish cannabis goods handling methods and evaluate all storage areas for potential cross-contamination issues. Keep a separate storage area for chemical cleaners and other hazardous materials. Check your local regulations regarding cannabis inventory and hazardous materials storage.

Provide Refrigeration

Commercial refrigeration is necessary for edibles. Buy a commercial refrigerator since typical consumer refrigerator models do not give you as even a temperature or ample enough room.

Waste and Recycling

Make sure you have an area where you can store cannabis waste for proper disposal. You cannot just throw away packages or people will raid your dumpster. Some provinces or states may enact new laws that make it illegal to throw cannabis waste in common dumpsters for this very reason.

Break Room

Employees often stand all day. If you want to keep your employees happy, have a small break room. Make sure it has a fridge and microwave so your employees can bring their lunches. Also make sure there is a sink and hot water. You can also choose to have a coffee pot with coffee ready.

Office and Security Monitoring Room

Every dispensary needs an office. It needs ample room and lighting, filing cabinets (with locks), and a desk and with chairs for two. One chair for you, the other for the employee you need to have a "serious" talk with. This room is more than just an office, it's a security monitoring room. It has a computer that keeps help you to keep track of your inventory and a wall of monitors to watch every inch of the dispensary.

Setup Your Vault

This is where all products and cash go at the end of the day. Make sure you have two safes in your vault, one for cash and one for products; otherwise your cash will smell like cannabis, and the banker will not be too happy.

Take Action

Location and interior design matters. The following should help you plan for your location and interior design needs:

- **Choose** several potential locations for your shop. Have a 'good neighbor' policy when it comes to choosing your location and try to meet the local business owners.

- **Read** the lease agreement with care. Hire an experienced lawyer to help you negotiate the lease agreement before signing.

- **Meet** an architect or interior designer, ideally one with experience in designing welcoming entrances, public areas and backrooms for dispensaries.

You have a lot of valuable products and cash on hand. You will need to think about your Security Plan to protect your business from expected and unforeseen threats.

L.A.
end

Chapter 8

Security is the Cost of Doing Business

"The media tends to glorify the cannabis industry and makes it seem everyone is printing money. In reality, it is far more difficult to operate a business in the cannabis industry than any other because of the unforeseen events that happen on a daily basis -- bank accounts getting shut down, policies changing at the state and federal level, in addition to the risks keeping talented employees out of the space."[135]

ISAAC DIETRICH, CEO OF MASSROOTS, A PUBLICLY TRADED CANNABIS SOCIAL MEDIA PLATFORM

"Everyone in the industry is having nightmares," said Michael Elliot, executive director of the Marijuana Industry Group in Colorado. "You hit a 7-Eleven, you'll get 20 bucks. You hit a dispensary, you'll get $300,000 on a good day," adds Mitch Morrissey, District Attorney for Denver.[136]

Lauren Pelley writer of CBC News reported that some "dispensaries in Toronto make up to $30,000 a day. With thousands of dollars in cash and valuable inventory on hand, you better believe that crime is a big concern. Pelley writes, "'Employees and customers have been stabbed, pistol whipped and pepper sprayed,' said Toronto police Superintendent Bryce Evans, after a string of cannabis store robberies in early 2017. 'There's no doubt that the employees and customers had been traumatized by these violent armed robberies.'"[137] How prepared are you for an armed robbery? How about in-house theft? Shoplifters? Do you have the insurance protection you need? Having a Security Plan is a critical component of your Business Plan.

Security and Cannabis Laws

It is worth repeating, if you don't follow the rules, your shop can be shut down. The goal of Canada's *Cannabis Act* and those of the eight states to have legalized recreational cannabis is to "protect public health and public safety" and to "reduce criminal activities." There is a need to "protect children" and to prevent the "risk of cannabis diverted to an illicit market". If the City Inspector suspects any criminal activities or the breaking of any of the cannabis laws or regulations, he or she will fine you or shut you down.

Most applications for a business license will require a Security Plan to show:

- Police checks for the applicant and every on-site manager,

- Proof of a security alarm and fire alarm system contract,

- Proof of ownership or legal possession of the premises (written consent of landlord if leased),

- Plan to install video surveillance cameras,

- Plan for removing valuables from the business premises, an

- Plan for a safe on the premises.

Other conditions may also apply, such as restrictions on where a shop can be located (e.g. not within 1,000 feet of a school, recreation centre or youth centre).

Your employees will also have to follow the laws. They must ask for photo identification without fail when a customer buys marijuana, making sure the person is of the minimum age and the expiration date is current. If employees choose not to follow the rules by the book (such as disregarding laws not to use cannabis on or near the premises), then you could lose your business license.

Theft and the Black Market

The fact that you have cannabis products and a large sum of money on hand and in a safe close by makes you a target for criminals. In a typical robbery, criminals can take $20,000 to $50,000 from a dispensary, compared to $769 from convenience stores and $7,500 from a bank.[138] If you own a cannabis-related business, expect it to get robbed every two years.[139] Denver Police found in 2009 that 16.9 percent of dispensaries had been robbed.[140] The most violent robbery happened in 2010, a gunman in California forced two workers to the ground and shots them in the heads.

Thieves like to target dispensaries because of the high resale value of cannabis on the black market and the large holdings of cash that can be grabbed. SIVA Enterprises, a business that provides consulting, turnkey management, venture opportunities, and brand acquisitions and licensing, to cannabis entrepreneurs across the US, pinpointed the most typical robberies you will see:

- **Counter theft.** Dispensaries may hold four or five pounds of cannabis behind the counter, adding up to 10 to 20 thousand dollars' worth of products that thieves could steal at gunpoint.

- **Smash-and-grab attacks.** Thieves can crash through storefronts or break into a back window to grab whatever inventory is available.

- **Internal theft.** Cannabis store employees have the insider knowledge to how operations work to find ways to steal without detection.

Black market growers, however, will find it harder to survive legalization. "I actually have a lower cost of production than the criminals do, and it's because there are economies of scale," said Canopy Growth founder Bruce Linton, adding that organized crime may even see its production costs go up if police interrupt that supply chain from time to time.[141]

Even at the selling price of its low $5 a gram True Compassionate Pricing[142] for low-income medical patients and at a cost of $2.30 a gram[143] to produce, Canopy Growth makes a profit. On the service level, the black market is competing against same-day shipping from legal producers. On quality, the legal market offers pesticide-free, mold-free, more selection, and in some cases vegan-line or organic products. Higher quality, service delivery and lower prices are hard to compete against.

Establish a Security Plan

With the possible threats of crime in a business susceptible to a robbery, having a Security Plan is more important than ever. For many businesses starting out and juggling finances, a robbery can mean the difference between staying open or being permanently closing. Having a robust Security Plan reduces your chances of becoming the next victim. Having good security also helps to lower your insurance premiums. Here are a few ideas to make a burglary harder to accomplish.

Build Relations with Law Enforcement

It is always a good idea to have a positive relationship with the police. Police will visit the store to check that you complying with the laws, such as making sure you are not selling to those under the minimum age. Consider having the store manager act as a liaison person to actively maintain that positive relationship with the police department.

risky but maybe

Invite a law enforcement officer to walk through your dispensary for a tour from time to time. This not only sets the tone for customers and employees alike that they are in a safe place, it also helps to build that relationship with your local police.

Location also matters to thieves. For instance, the closer your dispensary is to a police station, the quicker the response for help. If at all possible, open your shop near a police station.

Add Alarms and Video Surveillance

The most effective way to protect your dispensary against a robbery or fire is to install an alarm system. Make no mistake, a security and fire alarm system is a requirement, not a choice. In Victoria, security systems in dispensaries "must be installed and monitored at all times." The best security systems include infrared sensors, ultrasonic detectors and surveillance cameras. You can set up motion detectors and sensors to detect entry through ceilings and floors, cameras to cover every aspect of your property, and for the extra cautious, panic buttons for gunpoint robberies.

yes

100%

Set up your video surveillance cameras around the entrance doors. Meet with the security company to install a monitoring alarm, so you know the monitoring center will receive immediate notice whenever someone enters at an unusual hour.

Check with your Fire Inspector about your dispensary's fire-detection and suppression requirements, who may also direct you to a reputable fire and security service company.

Hire Professional Security

can hire
sep.
alarm
co. +
security
co. if
wanted

Many business owners choose to hire a security service company to leave this work with the professionals. They take care of everything from the design, installation, and monitoring. Depending on your budget, this may be worth checking out. Security companies can offer an affordable monthly fee.

Some security service companies can also provide other services, including guard service in the lounge area and a guarded escort service to the bank. Beefing up your daytime security with experienced security guards offers peace of mind. Employees and customers will feel better knowing the presence of a security guard is helping to deter a robbery. Hire a security guard company whose guards are experienced working in stressful and potentially violent situations. The security guard company must, of course, be bonded, licensed and insured.

Perform Employee Background Checks

In any business, it is important to hire people you can trust. As an employer, do a criminal background checks on all your employees before you hire them. Depending on the cash handling needs of your dispensary, you should also do a credit check. (More on this in *Chapter 8: Hire, Train and Reward*.)

All higher up
staff should
get credit checked

Keep the Exterior Clear

Setting up the exterior can slow the incidents of crime.

Setup Lighting

Proper lighting inside and outside of the building will do a lot to deter crime. Dark spots around the building will hide places where people can enter the building. Make sure to put bright lighting around the doors and in areas that are difficult to see from the street. If you see a burnt out light bulb, replace it immediately. For added protection, put your lights on timers so that you never forget to turn them on.

Clear Exterior

Cars and dumpsters close the building are great place to hide in or beside. If at all possible, avoid putting the trash bin next to the building. Keeping trees and shrubs trimmed and away from windows and doors.

Limit Access

Putting up obstacles to enter the store will deter robberies.

Solid Secure Doors

Lock all exterior doors with a deadbolt lock (Grade 1 or 2, solid metal with no exposed screws on the exterior) and a throw bolt (the bolt that comes out of the door) at least 1 inch (2.5-cm) long.

Keys Offer Security

As soon as you occupy the building, hire a registered locksmith to re-key the locks. The locksmith will give you keys with its own identification number and "Do Not Duplicate" stamped on it.

Give keys to staff on a "need to have" basis, allowing certain keys to open some doors but not others. If there is theft to an area of the building, you will know whose key had access.

Always re-key the locks every time a key-holding staff leaves or someone loses the keys. Alternatively, you could install an electronic push button (keyless) door lock. Managers can monitor arrival and departure times using independent entry codes for employees.

fob system works best =) keys for "main" doors too

Secure Valuable in a Vault

When choosing a safe for cash and inventory, buy one that has been tested by Underwriters Laboratories, Inc. The higher the Underwriters Laboratories rating, the more difficult to break in. The locksmith will recommend you periodically change the safe combinations. Of course, only give a few senior level people the vault codes. It is a good idea to secure the vault or the room the safe is kept in with a closed-circuit video camera. Buzzer doors for rooms with the safe will also restrict the ease of entry.

safe selection

Protective Windows

Cheaper?

Criminals love to see windows. Windows are perhaps the most vulnerable ways to break in. Purchase windows with tempered glass or with anti-break film. Install glass-break detectors on windows, which trigger alarms if broken. Cover any windows in the rear of the building with heavy metal grates. For added security, you can install bulletproof glass and acrylic counter windows, such as those seen in fast cash, payday loan buildings.

Not my fav

Safc Rooftop

People forget about the rooftop entrance. In most cases this can the easiest way to break in. Security bars should cover all rooftop hatchways, air ducts and air vents. If there is a rooftop door the Fire Inspectors agrees is unnecessary for entrance area, board it up and block the door. Skylights do add beauty with natural lighting, but security takes a priority. Put burglary-resistant glass and security bars or a steel grill over glass skylights. Board up the entire skylight area, if possible.

Prepare an Emergency Plan

Theft, floods, and fires do happen. Make sure you have an Emergency Plan that outlines the steps to follow in an emergency. Include in this plan all the important telephone numbers, such as for the police and emergency services. For more information, download a copy of the Business Emergency Plan at the U.S. FEMA website (https://www.fema.gov).

Make Available the Emergency Plan

Managers should make sure all employees know about the Emergency Plan and have access to it whenever they need. You should test your fire emergency plan twice a year; which, by the way, is what your local the fire department and insurance agency may require you do anyway to lower the risks.

Train Employee to Handle Situations

One of the most important responsibilities of your staff is to keep an eye out for suspicious people who set off red flags. Look out for people who try to avoid your gaze or otherwise behave suspiciously. Use your judgement.

all procedures should be put in SOP

Your staff should know to remain calm when something happens. If a robbery does happen, tell your employees that their life is more important than the cash or cannabis. No one needs to be a hero and chase or follow the thieves. Employees should not talk back, fight nor negotiate with the thief. Give them what they came for and let them go. Let the police handle the rest. As soon as it is safe, close the store and call 911. Let no one else into the store until the police arrive.

Prevent Retail Losses

Retailers call it shrinkage – you can call it theft. National Retail Security Survey reported that shrinkage costs almost 4 percent of annual retail sales, to which about 35 percent comes from employee theft and nearly 40 percent from shoplifting.[144]

The most common and easily avoidable employee-related administrative errors include:

- Putting an order in twice.

- Giving the wrong amount of change. *the only reason we should have shrinkage is if product goes bad or otherwise becomes unsellable!*

- Collecting the wrong amount of money.

- Not adding the order up correctly.[145] *that should be out of the ?*

The good news is that reliable point of sale (POS) systems and customer video surveillance systems deter these sorts of retail losses. As you will read below, also watch all your invoices and spot-check all inventory you receive. As a precaution, also always have at least two employees present at opening and closing the shop. These measures will go a long way in deterring theft.

Set up Cash Handling Procedures

No one person should handle all aspects of the cash handling process. You will need to document in the job description who has the authority to handle cash and what responsibilities each person will be allowed to do. If you want your budtender to only deal with customers, then that is all they should do and this must be made abundantly clear.

Designate one person to handle the register and cash, one person to keep track of the records, and one person to deposit the money into the safe. This handoff of duties allows each employee to keep track of the other person's actions.

check + balance system

Catch Problems at Point-of-Sales

The most common place for employee theft to happen is at the POS terminal, where a cashier gives a customer (a friend) a discount, creates a fake return or simply removes cash from the register. The good news is that modern POS systems do an amazing job of sending automatic alerts when it detects an exception. However, it is worthwhile having a cash handling procedure in place to reduce this threat.

Begin by separating the duties and knowing that every transaction is being recorded. For example, dispensaries should not allow employees to have more than a certain amount of cash in the registers during their shift. This cuts down on losses in a robbery and reduces the temptation for employees to steal. Managers should check receipts every couple of hours based on your dispensary's active sales. Everything has to match sales and receipts – this is the main responsibility of the manager on duty. If this basic system is followed, then workers are held responsible for shrinkage losses.

don't agree

Place Cash in a Secure Location

I like this idea

Place excess cash in a secure location when you remove it from the cash drawer. One option is to seal each drawer's cash in an envelope and sign it, making it tougher for anyone to break the seal and forge a signature. Deposit that envelope into a safe, which should be located in a locked room. Keep a record of the times and dates of the deposits.

cash drops + procedures => include in SOP

L.A. End

Cashless Business

In October 2017, Hawaii became the first state to require all medical marijuana dispensaries to go cashless, in a bid to deter robberies that target dispensaries. Under this cashless system, customers use their checking accounts to pay CanPay, which sends the payment to Safe Harbor, a Hawaii-based credit union.[146] This is a revolutionary idea in a country where banks fear dealing with this industry.

This does not affect Canada, but CanPay does introduce an interesting idea for dealing with the problem of holding a large amount of cash. Perhaps one day soon apps like CanPay will become more common. CanPay is already an option in six states, including California and Colorado.

At the time of this writing, there is still uncertainty about how the US federal government will react to this development in Hawaii. Attorney General Jeff Sessions may begin to crack down on the legal marijuana industry and several bugs still need to be worked out in this cashless system (e.g. how to include those without checking accounts or smartphones).

Watch Your Inventory

You won't catch all theft, but if you consistently apply the rules, you set the tone and every now and then you find something to correct.

Limit Belongings to Restricted Areas

Ideally, no employee ever steals from the business. But realistically, temptation is ever-present. One of the reasons most employees work around cannabis is because they use it themselves. Maybe someone wants to sell it on the black market.

A few things you can do to reduce this sort of theft is to follow some precautions. Managers must never allow personal bags or objects of the employees near the counters or inventory storage area. Tell employees that all jackets, boots, and bags must only be kept in designated area. You can also incentivize honesty by offering an "employee discount". It also helps to pay them well.

Of course, your employees deserve to be trusted and shown respect. Do not be so obsessed with catching a potential thief that you treat them like criminals and with disrespect.

Conduct Inventory Audits

Managers should check invoices every day for items delivered into inventory. Conduct a random inventory count of a particular item and compare it to the sales of that period. Checks that all items signed off as delivered are actually in storage. The number of items you start with, plus the number you received in deliveries, minus the amount signed out by staff, must equal inventories on hand. If there is a discrepancy, you may have a thief.

Monitor Trash Disposal

All sorts of outside garbage pails or debris near the building can offer opportunities for a thief. A dishonest employee can stash a product in the garbage and then grab it after work. Managers must check trash and have a system in place to monitor disposal. Using clear garbage bags is one way to limit employees from hiding products in the trash.

Setup Cybersecurity

Computer security (also known as cybersecurity) is the protection of your dispensary's computer system from theft or damage to your hardware, software or information, or from the disruption or misdirection of the services.

Two major cyber-attacks in the industry have already happened. The first major hack hit a medical marijuana dispensary in Nevada in December 2016. Hackers stole information about Nevada Division of Public and Behavioral Health's business, its employees, and data on more than 11,000 medical marijuana applicants. The second major hack came two weeks later. This time to the national database of MJ Freeway, a major POS systems company. The MJ Freeway hack disabled POS systems for medical marijuana dispensaries across the United States. "It's still an active investigation with a third-party IT firm and we'll pursue potential criminal action, so we're keeping the details reserved", said Jeannette Ward, director of data and marketing at MJ Freeway.[147]

It may cost you extra, but hiring a security expert to feel secure that your retail store's computer systems is protected, protects you and your customers.

Select the Right Insurance

As a business owner, you know the value of protecting your family, your staff, and yourself. Better security means lower insurance premiums. Insurance in the legal marijuana industry is still at its early stages of development. Several major carriers are emerging to provide coverage at an affordable cost. Start by finding three insurance companies favorable to the marijuana industry. Whatever you do, remember that whoever is writing your insurance policies is doing so because he or she earns commissions on these policies. You should shop around, negotiate, and always be on the lookout for a better deal.

Liability Insurance

General liability is a must-have for your dispensary. Liability insurance protects your business from losses due to bodily injury that happens to others in your store or damage to other's property. It also covers the injured person's medical expenses, your lawyer fees and expenses during legal proceedings.

"This is unprecedented and unchartered territory and nobody knows what the risks are ahead of us. It makes sense for state and local governments to require liability insurance to protect the public," said Matt Gunther, a Washington-based construction insurance broker.[148]

Business Property Insurance

Property insurance protects your building, inventory, and equipment from losses or damage due to theft, accidents or other unforeseen incidents. Depending on if you own or lease the property, coverage could include the building's structure, furniture, fixtures and tenant improvements.

Key Person Insurance

You might want to consider this coverage for your dispensary manager. Most small businesses depend on a few key people. If there is a loss of this person (no matter how temporary), this could devastate your dispensary. If the key person becomes injured or ill, and is unable to work, this policy does offer some protections.

Workers' Compensation Insurance

If you have employees, you are required to have Worker's Compensation coverage. If an employee is injured at work – fault or no fault of yours – Workers' Compensation Insurance will cover your legal costs and lawsuit penalties.

Product Coverage

prob. don't need?

Product liability covers all edible marijuana, vaporizing tools and smoking devices. This protects your dispensary from loss due to illness or injury to someone from a manufactured cannabis product (e.g. the consumption of edibles presents a concern).

Although this policy applies mostly to cannabis-infused edibles manufacturers who deal with carriers, dispensaries and select product manufacturers to deliver products, retail dispensary should think about protecting themselves should something tamper with your products while in transit.

Prob don't need it's cheap enough can't hurt!

"Up to this point, no edible cannabis product manufacturers maintained any product liability coverage," said Michael Aberle, national director, MMD Insurance Services. "If a dispensary sold a product to a patient, and that patient was to become ill or die as a result of consuming the product, the dispensary where the product was purchased, as well as the wholesaler and manufacturer, could be held liable."[149]

Business Income Insurance

One type of coverage that many business owners overlook is loss of income. If the policyholder gets sick or injured, or there is a business disruption such from a fire, theft or accident, loss of income coverage could make the difference between a few days' sick or closing your doors all together. This covers rent, utilities, and payroll, and could cover losses if you have to move to another location after a fire.

L.A.
end

Take Action

Security is the cost of doing business. Robbery and employee theft are concerns. The following should help as you prepare your Security Plans:

- **Write** a Security Plan. Look for security service companies that can help you set up an Emergency Plan, video surveillance and alarms, and security systems.

- **Establish** cash handling procedures and use your POS system to check for irregularities.

- **Choose** the insurance that is right for you and your business. At the very least, buy fire, liability and workers' compensation insurance. Product liability is desirable. A discussion with an agent will help to find the insurance policy right for you.

- **Hire** a cybersecurity expert to set up your network systems to protect your data.

In this industry, customers judge you on how your staff treat them. How well prepared are you with your hiring practices to ensure you can trust and find the most qualified employees?

Chapter 9

Hire, Train and Reward

"Be prepared to deal with perhaps the most diverse spectrum of personalities an industry has ever known. The cannabis space has luminaries with M.B.A.s, Ph.D.s, and J.D.s, but just as many with no formal education whatsoever. Expand your lexicon so that you are fluent in both boardroom and barroom, because to be successful, you'll need to be well versed in both."[150]

SASHA KADEY, CHIEF MARKETING OFFICER OF GREENLANE, OWNER OF THE LARGEST VAPORIZER DISTRIBUTOR IN NORTH AMERICA, VAPEWORLD

Having great employees start with being a great boss. Customers will judge your dispensary by the competence of your staff. Your business is only as good as the people who interact with your customers. While employees may sweep the floors or restock the shelves, their primary duty is to wait on customers in a courteous, friendly and helpful manner. Everything else becomes secondary when a customer walks in. From the weekend cashier to the head budtender, every employee plays a vital role.

Hiring and the Cannabis Laws

Many people mistakenly believe that all you need to have to work in the industry is an interest in cannabis. While it is important, a lot of the retail cannabis work comes down to showing basic customer service skills. First-time customers will come into your retail dispensary and not know what they want. Having a positive (or negative) interaction with your staff will change the entire experience for them.

Employees are required "to protect public health and public safety". In particular, employees must:

- Only serve those at or above minimum age (21 in the U.S. and 18 or 19 in Canada),

- Deter criminal activities and recognize the sanctions and enforcement measures,

- Provide access to a quality-controlled supply of cannabis (contaminant-free), and

- Enhance public awareness of the health risks associated with cannabis use.

Simply put, employees need to follow the law. Other rules will surely apply (e.g. no consumption on or near the premises), which the employee must be made aware of. Police currently raid "unlicensed" cannabis dispensaries. Undercover police walk into dispensaries to check whether employees ask for identification or medical documents.

"Police have said in the past they won't bust unlicensed pot shops unless they are found to be selling to minors, involve violent activities or are connected to organized crime," wrote Vancouver Sun's Yvonne Zacharias.[151] Nevertheless, employees have done this, following in fines and shut downs. An example of this happened in April 2015, when Vancouver's Weeds Glass + Gifts cannabis shop served an underage customer on one occasion. The owner went to court and was found guilty.

Employees must act in a manner that there is:

- No risk to public health or safety, including the risk of cannabis diverted to an illicit market or activity.

- No false or misleading information knowingly told to customers or regulators.

- No violation of cannabis laws, federal drug laws or food and safety laws.

Said another way, the City Inspector is watching. He or she must have no reason to suspect any criminal activities. Your dispensary needs to show that it is crime-free.

Legal Limitations

factor onboarding fees => background + drug test prices

Managers no doubt will want to use any means to protect the business from employee theft. No manager or employee wants to deal with violence or an unsafe workplace. Some employers go the extra distance requiring credit checks and criminal background checks, banning anyone who has a hint of a questionable past. There is good reason to believe this a dangerous way to think.

Marcus Richardson is, in the eyes of the law, a criminal. In fact, a convicted drug trafficker. In 1998, Richardson, a member of the B.C. Compassion Club Society, drove across Vancouver's Lions Gate Bridge and was stopped at a roadblock by police. They found several kilograms of cannabis and $6,000 in his trunk.[152] The money he carried was to pay the growers. The judge convicted him for trafficking. Today, a father of three, he holds a federal license to grow and runs a business selling equipment for medical cannabis users.

Would you hire him? Probably. There is nothing criminal about him and he knows a lot about cannabis for medical purposes. American companies call him to share his expertise, but he can't cross the border. He wants to volunteer for his kids 'field trips' but the school conducts a criminal check. "I wouldn't want to embarrass my children."[153]

Now consider if you hired him – a judgement call – and not someone else equally qualified and with the same conviction. Perhaps for a different set of circumstances, someone from an aboriginal community or a well-known poor city neighborhood – another judgement call. Would you be in the right? Hard to say. Simply put, you cannot refuse to hire someone unless you can prove their criminal conviction has a direct impact on the ability to do their job.

Racism, sexism, homophobia, religious intolerance, discrimination, call it what you will, but it does show up in an interview – consciously or unconsciously. Government employment agencies have long recognized that arrest rates disproportionately affected lower income and minority groups. Having a criminal record or poor credit history should not bar you from getting a job. Many federal and state/provincial lawmakers agree.

The first thing an employer needs to do is to get advice from a lawyer about the laws that apply to the area. Better yet, Catherine Morisset of Marijuana Venture advises that you "have your lawyer review any job applications, background check authorizations and any questionnaires the employer intend to have prospective employees complete. If the laws in your area permit these checks, then you have to show it is 'substantially job-related' in writing."[154] The subtleties of what makes employment laws in one jurisdiction different from another are best left in the hands of a lawyer.

The Value of Employees

[handwritten margin notes: create clear terms of employment; equal opport. employer; L.A. start; TO packs exblity ructure der ar ules + pectations; osts]

Hiring and retaining the right employee has a direct impact on the profitability and effectiveness of your dispensary. Employees directly control access to the products and the presentation of your dispensary. It is surprising how many managers fail to offer proper training or an enjoyable atmosphere that can make the job easier.

An unmotivated employee is not as effective as a satisfied one. Just as word-of-mouth is your dispensary's best advertising, negative comments from an employee about the products or owners can turn customers off. Your products could be great but a rude cashier can also turn customers away. There is absolutely nothing stopping a customer from taking their business elsewhere.

According to the American Management Association, this cost of replacing an employee can be up to 30 percent of that position's annual salary.[155] The costs of placing a job ad, the interviewer's time, security check, training mistakes, and the labour hours spent by the employee before reaching a productive level add up.

Finding a top-notch employee is in limited supply. You are competing a little bit every day with the dispensary next-door to attract the right people. The best advice from the start is to pay your employees a living wage, offer benefits and show them the respect they deserve for their talents and ideas.

Hiring Retail Cannabis Employees

The most important consideration when hiring someone is deciding whether the rest of the team would want to work 10 or

12 hours a day next to this person. If there is any doubt, do not hire this person} Your staff are an important part of your business, so it is essential you find the right fit. The following sections describe the steps involved in hiring the right people, working with them, and knowing when to say "good-bye".

Write a Job Description

Every dispensary is unique. It cannot be overstated but before you hire your first employee, write a job description. If you do not know what that job is about, you will not find the right person for the job. The three most important positions to hire are budtender, cashier and store manager. Take your time in understand their roles and responsibilities.

DA /**Budtender.** The budtender role is the most rewarding and sometimes the most challenging position because they are ones building a direct relationship with your customers. In marijuana clinics, patients spend 90 percent or more of their time interacting with just one person: the budtender.[156] Which makes this position the most important one inside your dispensary. The best budtenders are passionate about cannabis, knowledgeable about the products, and strive to provide great customer service. A good attitude and strong work ethic are the keys to success for this position.

DA's typically do the cash too

Cashier. Cashiers work next to budtenders. They listen first-hand to the knowledge imparted to customers and watch in the delivery of customer services. The cashier is a good quick option when looking for a new budtender. But if this move from cashier to budtender happens, keep this new budtender away from the cash handling duties.

if marketing or general or sales
↳ *we'll have multiple who oversee diff. specialties*

↰ **Manager.** The key to success in this position is a manger who stays on top of things and does not let things go until tomorrow. The duties could include (but not limited to):

- Acting as media contact and staying abreast of industry news

- Controlling waste and product costs (includes daily budgets, inventory)

- Customer education, consultation and product recommendations

- Enhancing employee communications and morale

- Establishing and maintaining product quality control

- Health and safety regulation enforcement

- Hiring, training, supervising and scheduling employees

- Key holder responsibilities to help open and close

- Leadership around sales, operations, customer, and community and staff engagement

- Meeting with store suppliers and sales representatives

- Ordering, receiving, storing and issuing all products

- Keeping the owner informed of problem areas

- Keeping up with social media and marketing plans

- Staying current on all cannabis law regulations

- Setting safety standards, training employees and complying with regulations

Set Occupational Requirements

In many states and provinces, it is illegal to single out a particular candidate for a background check. Instead, you should interview and consider all applicants equally; only then can you run a background check. You cannot simply deny a person a position because of a conviction unless it is relate to the job. For instance, a criminal conviction for drug dealing or theft is relevant if a position that requires inventory controls and cash handing, but a DUI conviction is not, if the job involves no driving.[157] A person with a troubled past could have changed his or her life around. In some cases, if you see arrests "not subject to prosecution", it could mean the person was innocent or wrongly accused. Be careful, misinterpretations and misunderstandings do happen.

Which is why you need to create a list of 'occupational requirements.' This involves writing an outline of the areas of the job that – if a convicted criminal ran the operations – would jeopardize the role. This first means writing out the job description and then writing out a list of relevant convictions for denying an applicant for the job.[158] It is even better if you can make your decision based on statistics. For example, an applicant with a theft conviction is more likely to steal than an applicant without one. You need to explain how denying a position to someone because of a conviction relates to the performance of the job.

Mikal Belicove of Forbes Magazine advises, "Do be consistent. Ensure that the process for all applicants is consistent. Two applicants applying for the same job should have the same searches and investigations run on them. Different job types may require different levels of investigation, but for the same job title, make sure you keep your process uniform to avoid charges of discrimination[159]

Keep in mind that you cannot perform a background check before a job has been offered, only after a job offer is made[160] Since a background check takes time, start your new hire search early so you have enough time to make a conditional offer during the hiring process. *[L.A. stop]*

Pre-Screen Employees *Read/ once into review hiring process*

Screening people before you schedule an interview will save you time and help to reject any obviously unsuitable people from the start. Someone who is knowledgeable about the dispensary's employment needs should do this preliminary screening. When looking through resumes, consider the following questions:

- **Leadership qualities.** Is the person an achiever and doer, or an individual who needs direction? Look at past employment positions and promotion growth rates.

- **Determination.** Does the person finish what he or she starts? Does he or she look for (or retreat from) challenges. Examine time at school and at their last job.

- **Stability.** You do not want employees to leave in two months. Look at past employment dates. Job stability can also be a window into a candidate's emotional makeup.

- **Experience.** Is the person qualified to do the job? Examine past job experience.

Conduct the Interview

Interviewers must set the example and come to the interview on time. They must also thoroughly know the job offered. Interviewers should conduct the entire interview in private and try help to make the applicant feel at ease. Try to make sure the person interviewed has answered all of your questions. Whenever possible, let the applicant speak. Never reveal that you disapprove of an answer, even if you do.

Consider the following questions for the interview:

- **Motivation.** Why are you applying at this dispensary? Why at all in the cannabis industry? Is your decision career-related or temporary? Does your motivation come from within or some outside pressure (e.g. spouse or parent)?

- **Maturity.** Will you be able to relate with other employees and customers who may be older? Is the individual mature enough to work in a stressful environment?

- **Work habits.** Are you aware of the physical demands involved with lifting and standing? Have you done similar work?

- **Personality.** Do you have the type of personality that shows good customer service and will complement with other employees?

- **Availability.** Can you easily commute? Can you work the hours expected?

Ask a few questions they do not expect, such as "what is your favorite movie?" In all of the questions, try to understand their attitude and interests.

Another great way to test knowledge and personality is to role-play. You, the interviewer, acts as a customer with specific needs. If interviewing a budtender, role-play with these two questions in mind: 1) Which strains are better for a specific aliment (e.g. sleep, arthritis, appetite)? 2) Which strains are good for certain effects (e.g. concentration, socializing)? Listen to what the candidate recommends to guide you, the customer, towards the right choice.

Conduct Criminal Background Check

It is time to hire. This means checking the references and screening for signs of trouble. Take 30 minutes to call the references – this is normal and just plain good hiring practice. Let's be clear, although reference checking is permissible, this is not the same as a credit check or a criminal background check.

Since it takes time to do a background check, give a 'conditional' offer to the applicant. Also make it clear that any conditional offer will depends on the results of the background check. Under federal and state/provincial laws, employers may be required to give the applicant notice that they intend to reject an application based on a conviction, along with an explanation.

Before you perform a credit or a criminal background check, you must get the applicant's written consent. Let applicants know what information you are looking for and why. Based on the way the background check is conducted, you will be required to have a legal release form completed by the applicant, inform that person of his or her rights, and provide that applicant with a copy of the report, as well as adverse actions communications.[161]

To conduct a background check, hiring a screening company can do a far better job of locating the information you need. These third-party businesses have the experience and know the processes, and prevent you from viewing data that might run you afoul of your state/provincial or federal laws.

After learning about an applicant's criminal conviction, take care in how you interpret any of the information. Catherine Morisset of Marijuana Ventures advises you to consider:

- nature and gravity of the offense;
- time that passed since the offense; and
- nature of the job.

You should consider the applicant's age at the time of conviction. Look for signs the individual performed the same type of work being hired for after the conviction, with no incidents of criminal conduct. [162] It is also helpful to look at the length and consistency of employment history before and after the offense. Did the applicant go through any rehabilitation, such as education and training? What other positions and information shows this person's fitness for the particular job?

Paul Gerber of the Cannabis Business Executive advises you to "only consider denying candidates who have been convicted or have pending prosecutions. In most cases, a crime committed 10 or more years ago, even if it is relevant to the job, does not pose as much of a serious risk. Studies have shown that most repeat arrests occur within 3 years of the first conviction."[163]

Catherine Morisset of Marijuana Ventures suggests that if you find something on a background check that may affect your decision to hire an applicant, you should – at a minimum – engage in a conversation with the applicant. So many misconceptions, mistakes, and reporting errors can be resolved by conducting that face-to-face communication.[164] Remember to keep all the details on the background check confidential. People have a right to their privacy.

Reject Applicants in a Positive Way

Rejecting people for a job is the unpleasant of the job hiring process. If any of the applicants are qualified but you could not hire them for one reason or another, ask them for permission to contact them again when another opening becomes available. If they accept, put their names into a 'prospective applicant file'. But be careful not to make it appear that they will be hired.

Some people will ask for a reason to why they were rejected. Explain only what is necessary to settle the person's questions. Usually it is enough to say, "We accepted an applicant who was better qualified" or "who has more experience." Always be honest, but tactful.

Make the Final Decision

You may have more than one qualified person for the job, but which one do you decide on? Always base your decision of who to hire on the total picture the person presented throughout the application process. Consider the person's education, employment, criminal history, and social media. Cannabis dispensaries lose great candidates when they look at only one specific item. Get advice from those who were also involved in the interview or had contact with the applicant.

When you do offer the position, make sure the applicant fully understands the following terms and conditions of the job before accepting the position:

- Job description

- Start date

- Salary

- What to wear

Whomever you choose, select someone you feel good about having around. Someone you will enjoy working with and feel has a very good chance of being successful at the job.

Sign the Employee Agreement

In this new industry, you might have a trade secret. Maybe you have a better way to train employees written out in a training manual. Maybe it is a better way to operate your sales and inventory systems that generates even more profit. What happens when one of your employees quits and starts to work for a competing dispensary, taking with him or her all of your confidential information?

From day one, have the new hire read an employment agreement and sign it. The employment agreement must also describe the duties and responsibilities expected for the job. For instance, it is against the law for recreational use on the premise and it could shut you down. If the employee is a recreational user, tell them they cannot use cannabis during working hours. Tell them it is like a bartender drinking on the job.

Also explain to the new hire that if he or she is caught stealing just once, they are fired and the police will be called in. This way, there is no surprise when it does happen.

When it comes to protecting your confidential information or trade secrets, talk to your lawyer about drafting into the contract a non-disclosure agreement that protects you.

Create Personnel Files

Set up a personnel file once the applicant is hired. Include the following information:

- Name, address and phone number

- Social Insurance Number

- Emergency contact information

- Job title and pay rate

- Employment date

- Past performance evaluations

- Termination date and the reason for termination

Good record keeping helps you remember the details about an employee when you need them.

Day-to-Day Operations

The fastest way for a retail cannabis store to lose credibility is for its staff to give out bad advice or to 'push products'. Word gets out fast, if your staff do not know what they are talking about. You cannot 'fake it till you make it'. Only recommend products that are appropriate to the customer, based on the best available information. The most important investment you will ever make is in training. They need to know the strains and products from the start. They are the face of your dispensary.

Deliver In-House Training

One serious problem today is the lack of industry training and education. New employees jump into a job with little to no formal training. Some lack the basic knowledge about cannabis, such as its health benefits, strain names, CBD and THC mg serving sizes. On the job, they scramble to get whatever bits of information and skills they can, whether correct or not. Poor recommendations can harm medical customers and damage your business's reputation. If employees do not know the products, how can you expect them to educate your customers?

Find a good in-house trainer. Ideally, the employee's regular supervisor should do all the training. The trainer must be knowledgeable about and experienced in the job, a model employee able to communicate, and with a great deal of patience and understanding. The most effective training is hands-on training, getting the new employee to do something their work involves. For example, show them how to replace a vape cartridge. Keep in mind that training is far more than teaching a skill. Managers will need to look beyond their own interests and consider the employee's interests and talents.

Create an employee handbook. Give the new employee a copy of the employee manual that outlines the days off and business's rules. After taking their time to read it, have them sign the "I have read and understand" commitment attached to the manual. The employee handbook need only be a few pages. This handbook helps your staff to know the important on-the-job rules from day one.

Prepare a 30-minute orientation and training schedule. An employee orientation is a key part of any the first day job training. The basic orientation plan should introduce the new employee to the owners, the business setup, other employees and supervisors. From the start, set up a schedule for the training you need to provide and the dates you expect activities to start and finish.

Start with a shift meeting. You only have three goals for a shift meeting: generate a positive group feeling, start a dialogue, and training. Pre-shift meetings should last no more than 15-minutes. Ideally, you should hold a quick staff meeting before every shift, every day, to explain daily specials, upcoming events, and to put everyone in a positive mood. Longer, more complicated meetings – such as for product safety training – should be scheduled for 'after hours' to allow more time and open discussion.

Outside Help in Training

If you employ several people, you might find it helpful to contact outside support to come to one of your meetings.

Look for experts in their fields. Look for people who are genuinely interested in sharing their wisdom. Often just a phone call is enough. Here are some ideas for speakers to invite:

- City Health Department Inspector - edible safety practices and requirements

- Edible vendor sales rep. - food safety, ingredients and production process

- Product vendor sales rep. – features and benefits of product and customer needs

- Software vendor salesperson – POS and security needs

- Security vendor salesperson – security practices and requirements

- Community Services police officer – crime prevention and response tips

- Bank trainer – proper cash-handling techniques

- Red Cross instructor – basic first aid and CPR

- Health organizations – medical / health information

- Farmer (cultivator) – Nature, cannabis botanical and chemical science

- Lab testing professional – methods, quality and consistency of cannabis products

Use training resources. Eventually, a national certification standard will emerge. But until then, be careful with 'budtender certification' programs (at least for now). While existing programs offer a well-thought out curriculum, some fail to prepare you for the work involved. Here are a few paid resources available to assist with training.

- THC University (thcuniversity.org)

- Cannabis-Training-University (cannabistraininguniversity.com)

- Oaksterdam University (oaksterdamuniversity.com)

- Cannabis College (cannabiscollege.com)

Evaluate Performance

Evaluating your employee's job performance is a crucial step in growing your business. Mangers have to be aware of an employee's strengths, so as to know which areas the employee can improve on and how the manager can help. Managers need to be able to impart all the skills and attitude needed for the job in a way that gets employees excited about serving customers.

Job training and scheduled performance reviews will help to keep the lines of communication open and promote a good spirit of teamwork. Quarterly, one-on-one performance evaluation meetings will help to break down any communication barriers between management and employees.

Remember that evaluations are only part of a communication process and should never be a substitute for regular, daily communication. You and your supervisory team must always be available to listen.

Offer Employee Rewards

A few incentive like offering discounts, grand prizes (e.g. gift cards), free food (e.g. pizza), or a personal paid time-off can do wonders in helping to motivate employees to reach targeted sales goals. The cost of rewards is small cost, but these little extras add up to big wins in low turnover rates and higher productivity.

To motivate individuals, you will need to set goals that reflect your business's values. Your customer service should not feel pushy or focused on making money, money, money. Focusing on the bottom line puts your customers as second best. This is not to say that suggestive selling does not work, but it must be done well.

It is true, the bigger the sale, the bigger the profits; but your staff should focus on serving the customer's needs. If a customer came back because of an exceptional selection and service to their needs, and told their friends and family, what would that experience be like? If instead, if they felt pressured to buy more expensive products or felt the experience was unpleasant, what would that feel like? In either case, which one do you think would have them come back time and again? Work on building customer loyalty, not just per sales average.

Set high enough (yet realistic enough) goals for daily, weekly and monthly sales targets. To track and coach individuals, managers should plan for 30-minute weekly or biweekly meetings with each individual on the front desk team. This is the time to review the employee's sales performance and make suggestions on how he or she can hit sales goals.

Telling your employees that their performance is valued in private meetings and showing them in public meetings are two entirely different things. By now, you should have a track record of their individual successes in sales. If you have regular 'all-dispensary team' meetings (and monthly meetings are recommended for building a healthy, strong team culture), remember to recognize the individuals who have achieved their goals and reward them in public. Show all of your employees that you value them as individuals and for their contributions towards the team.

Scheduling and the Launch Opening

The best management tool for controlling labour cost is proper scheduling. The main goal of scheduling is to put your best employees on shifts where they achieve the most productivity. Proper scheduling takes into account the peak hours and days in the week, the desires of each of employee for shifts and days off, and the skill levels of each employee.

During the first couple of months, be sure you have plenty of staff available since your dispensary could suddenly become busy. Take Maria Sharp's advice, a former budtender and dispensary manager, "Avoid opting for a slew of short shift employees instead of a strong core staff with a couple of part-timers to help fill gaps."[165] At the beginning, most customers will understand that you just opened and that not all of the bugs have worked out yet. Schedule your best employees to open to store, then the others at the times you need them.

Opening a business is a great test of your managerial abilities. Once you have the desired date for your opening, you will have plenty of work to do. To be on schedule, you will need help from your staff to decorate and set up the store. Try to delegate them some assignments. Keep track of who is assigned what, when and how. Allow plenty of time for your staff and yourself to finish since even the smallest tasks might open a hornet's nest of unforeseen problems and reasons for delay. It is vital at this time that you keep communications open with your key staff.

Saying Good-Bye

There are all sorts of reasons an employee might want to leave a business. The employee was fired, another job offered more pay, going back to school, you name it. There comes a time when you have to say "good bye".

Terminate an Employee

Firing someone is an unpleasant thing to do. After performance reviews and chances to improve, there are few other choices. You should reach your decision to fire an employee after weighing the pros and cons, never in anger, tired or under stress. Even though this is unpleasant to do, it must be done for the good of your business. Do not let this situation go on for more than 24-hours since it could be far worse to let the employee stay any longer.

Other employees may wonder why the individual was fired. Some may see this firing as a threat to their own job security. Sometimes you need to explain your reasons to soothe your team's concerns. In most cases though, the reasons will be obvious. Never share any derogatory thoughts or confidential information with your other employees about this individual. It is unprofessional and employees will lose respect and trust in you.

Conduct an Exit Interview

An exit interview is a valuable tool for everyone. You learn things about your operation that you were unaware of and can now correct. Your former employee can learn from you. Be honest with the employee about his or her performance and the reasons for the termination. Should the employee disagree, give him or her the opportunity to discuss the issue; but be sure you can back up your claims with a record of proven facts.

Take Action

Running a retail business is about making a personal connection, you with your staff and your staff with your customers. The following should help you prepare your plans for staffing:

- **Hire** employees you can trust and can work with others. There are so many ways a background check can go wrong. The rules concerning background checks will depending on where you live. Check with a lawyer to be sure you comply with the labour laws.

- **Establish** employee relations is about showing staff that you value them. This can mean paying them well and recognizing their talents and interests.

- **Train** employees with the help of in-house and outside trainers. This includes having an orientation on the first day of work for new staff.

- **Meet** with your staff regularly, such as daily shift-meetings, weekly one-on-one meeting, and quarterly performance evaluation meetings.

Hiring good staff will help to create that perfect place. You may have the right employees and the best products, but how to do you plan to reach your target customers?

Chapter 10
Marketing Your Business

"Since this store is clearly trying to be a weed store for the 1 percent, I asked Canto to show me their most luxurious products. He showed me a cigar made by Gold Leaf that costs $420 and contains 12 grams of flower and 4 grams of rosin oil. It's rolled in marijuana fan leaves, it smokes like a cigar, and it lasts for four to six hours. 'One of the smoothest things I've ever smoked on,' he said. A $400 cigar may seem a bit rich, but that was nothing. Canto pulled out a wooden box, lifted the lid, and showed me an even bigger cigar, also made by Gold Leaf, that costs $3,600. 'The cool thing about this cigar is they're one of a kind. This is for the consumer that wants to have an item that no one else has.' It contains 21 grams of flower and 7 grams of rosin oil. 'It's a very, very unique item,' he said. 'This is a memory that lasts forever.'"[166]

CHRISTOPHER FRIZZELLE, THE STRANGER, WRITING ABOUT ALEJANDRO CANTO, OWNER/COO OF DIEGO PELLICER

The cannabis industry is changing. From the increased demand for growing soils to chefs at gourmet restaurants perfecting their marijuana-infused chocolate cake. With so much expected to change, few know what this means. Will there be restrictions on "lifestyle" ads? Likely. Will TV and radio spots be off-limits? Probably. That is why dispensaries have to be up to date on the latest legal developments. It is hard to predict the packaging or health and safety regulations that will come. The rules for marketing are no different.

Marketing and the Cannabis Laws

Growing a business requires an ongoing effort to bring in new customers to your door. Marketing is an all-encompassing term that is any activity you do to present a message your customers will value, that helps them recognize your dispensary as the place to go. When it comes to marketing, cannabis laws want to prevent the spread of "false, misleading or deceptive information." Packaging, labels and lab testing go hand in hand with product quality. If clinical trial information is available, tell customers what you know. Otherwise, be careful what you say about the health claims and benefits that remain unproven.

The marketing rules for cannabis are still evolving. Most cannabis laws will have the following requirements:

General Requirements

- No deceptive, false or misleading statements.

- No communicating of the price or distribution.

- No advertising where it appeals to or seen by those below 21 years old.

- No testimonials or endorsements.

- No depiction of a person, character or animal, whether real or fictional.

- No presenting of brand element that evokes a positive or negative emotion about or image or a way of life that shows glamour, recreation, excitement, vitality, risk or daring.

- No giveaway coupons as promotional materials, or conduct promotional activities such as games or competitions to encourage sale of marijuana or marijuana products.

- No (or limited) sponsoring of events or facilities.

Broadcast Advertising

- Possible broadcast, cable, radio, and print communications. In California, you must prove to the local compliance officer that no more than 30 percent of the audience is expected to be under the age of 21.

- Possible for the Internet website (e.g. pop-up advertising). In California, you must prove to the local compliance officer that no more than 30 percent of the audience to your website is expected to be under the minimum age.

- No safety claims that says the government approves.

- No safety claims that says the testing facility approves.

Outdoor Advertising

- No leaflet or flier directly handed to any person in a public place.

- No advertising on or in a public transit vehicle or public transit shelters.

- No adverting on or in a publicly owned or operated property.

- No advertising within 1,000 feet of children, postsecondary campus or substance abuse facility.

Given these set of circumstances, you may also find that radio stations, TV ads and newspapers reluctant to work with you. Fear not, there is still a lot you can do.

Investing in Customers

So how much should you spend to acquire a new customer? There is no right or wrong answer. The key is to compare this cost against the lifetime value of a customer.

Determine the Customer Acquisition Cost

If your new customer came in, bought an edible and never came back, the money you spent to attract that customer will feel like a waste. That is why customer retention is so important. Let's use a simple example (below) with John Smith and his wife Mary. John is a new customer. John and his wife Mary have two growing girls. They just moved into your neighborhood.

Count advertising cost per walk-in customer. Let's say you spent $1000 in May and the number of individual sales was 100 people for the month. The basic formula for calculating customer acquisition cost is to divide your total advertising costs by the number of new customers. Your cost to acquire 100 new customers is $10 per customer. In this example, the acquisition cost for John was $10.

As a new business, every customer is new. So it will be easier to know your exact total advertising cost. To compare acquisition costs from month to month, divide your customer count by the actual advertising expenses from the opening to the end of the 30-day cycle. You can now compare current 30-day period to the prior month. After a year, you can compare the same month from this year with last year.

Count advertising cost per impression. Sometimes people need to see an ad 3 to 7 times before they notice you. This is often the case with print ads. Most people will see your ad but not notice it, while others will see it meets their needs to want to visit.

Let's say that John saw your ad in the local newspaper. It cost you $200 for a circulation of 10,000 people. Divide $200 by 10,000, that's a $0.02 cost per impression. Compare that with (say) your purchase of a regional magazine ad for $1000. Their circulation is 100,000. Divide $1000 by 100,000 for a $0.001 cost per impression.

All things being equal, your best value ad is the regional magazine, where you spend $1,000. However, if your $200 newspaper ad is in a special section that your target audience reads (say John), that ad would be a better value for your shop.

Know Your Customer's Lifetime Value

John likes to routinely buy dried bud, vape oil, two brownies, a beverage and a dozen, small mint candy each week for himself and his wife. John lives in your neighborhood for five years and plans to visit your shop every Friday afternoon after work.

CUSTOMER LIFETIME VALUE * Less 2-week vacation					
	Bud	**Vape Oil**	**2 Brownies**	**Beverage**	**Candy**
Weekly	$10	$7	$8	$6	$8
Annual	$500	$350	$400	$300	$400
5-Year 'Life'	$2,500	$1,750	$2,000	$1,500	$2,000

If John becomes a regular, that $10 acquisition cost per customer would be repaid 975 times over. Notice that John's total weekly spending is $39. This adds up over the five years to $9,750. Now multiply this by all your other weekly regulars. Of course, as a business you will spend more money on ads throughout the five years to keep John coming back, so the true returns are less dramatic. But you can see the point: advertising can be an investment.

Bringing In New Customers

Bringing in new customers is different from bringing in your regulars. For starters, it costs you about five times more to attract a new customer than it does to hold on to an existing one.[167] The question is how do you reach them?

In a new industry, do not be surprised if advertising is restricted at the beginning. Government-supported public awareness campaigns are your store's friend. The more people know, the easier it is to reach them. So many customers, so many questions. Your knowledgeable staff can help to answer some of these questions for curious visitors.

Your staff have to know what they are talking about. This translates into word-of-mouth as your best (and possibly only) tool for attracting new customers. According to Nielsen Media Research, 92 percent of consumers believe in recommendations that from friends and family over all forms of advertising.[168] This means you need to think of marketing in a different way – more targeted, more personal-feeling, and more informational.

Posters and Billboards

Let's say this up front: restrictions on print posters and billboard means that you cannot put your ads up anywhere where those under the minimum age can see it. Print advertising rules will depend on where you are located. That said, posters and billboards are fast becoming the darlings of cannabis business advertising in the United States, where cannabis ad billboards started by getting voters to support legalization. That changed in August 2014, when Dama unveiled more than a dozen ads across Seattle, becoming America's first-ever cannabis business to begin a billboard campaign.

The single worst thing any marketer can do is to promote cannabis as a product for hapless stoners. Dama's ads challenges this stereotype by showing an outdoorsy image. Seattle is a health-conscious, outdoorsy city, so this ad of two mountain hikers had better chance of catching attention. Of course, using this type of advertising will depend on what your jurisdiction allows. In Nevada, for example, cannabis dispensaries are free to advertise on casino coasters, billboards, flyers to hand out on the Vegas strip, and ads in a local magazines and newspapers. However, this might not happen the same in other jurisdictions. In Washington, for example, billboards can only show the name of the business, the nature of the business, and directional information.

Events and Presentations

Setting up exhibits at local events or even hosting your own event are great ways to drive traffic to your website and store visits. Higher Leaf in Seattle, for example, invites different growers every Friday to the store to offer an information session. Higher Leaf finds this is a good way to teach customers about their products.

If you do host events, offer free handouts, infographics, pens, tote bags, matchboxes, and coasters with your name, website and location. Put up signs to inform passerby of the event along with your contact information (of course, this depends on our local laws). Be sure to have a sign-up sheet ready and tell visitors about your newsletter.

Offer a Vibe Others Don't

Sometimes how a place looks or feels at the start can do the trick for bring in new customers. You could offer an espresso machine or coffee bar area (of course, this depends on your local laws). How about offering local or organic grown strains? Some dispensaries display artwork. You could put up several flat screen TVs along the walls for people to watch as they wait. How about offering cannabis-related magazine at the counters (even giving them away free)? Serving filtered water with a slice of lemon or watermelon could also do the trick. Sometimes it is the little things that get people talking.

Give Staff Something to Talk About

Sharing knowledge is the key to selling. New customers do not always know what they need. Let's say you offer the high-quality, locally crafted glass bongs. How do you get your customers to know? Having a great idea is not enough, you have to tell your customers about it. Give your staff the words to use in a conversation with customers.

Having knowledgeable staff who can explain the different products to customers will help you stand out. The more information your staff know, the more they can sell. Tips such as what happens if you eat too much edibles will be valuable for first-time users. You can also handout informational brochures over the counters.

Keep Customers Coming Back

The key to building monthly sales is to increase how much each regular customer buys. Obviously, how you relate to your customers will affect their opinion of you. If you can translate that opinion into customer loyalty, you will boost your bottom line.

In fact, a Bain & Company study found that a 5 percent increase in customer retention increased profits by 25 to 95 percent.[169] Those are might big return on investment. Said another way, all you need to do is to get your customers to come back one more time a month. If you offer good products and good customer service, you will soon have your regulars. For your bottom line to grow, focus on making your repeat customers happy – especially your most profitable ones.

Let Customers Know You Appreciate Them

As a manager, train new staff to remember who your regular customers are, their names and to take their time to remember faces. People love it when you remember who they are, making them feel valued. Consider having your staff wear nametags. When your staff get to know your customers by name, train them to look at customers as individuals, and to remember what they say and to observe what they prefer. How about setting up a customer "Wall of Fame" or giving your regulars "Outstanding

Customer" awards for their charitable work or contributions to the community? If you recognize customers and make them feel important, they will draw closer and hold a special place in their hearts for your store.

Clubs are a Great Way of Treating Your Regulars

National Access Cannabis, for example, offers cooking classes for its medical marijuana members. You could create a club that offers privileges or paraphernalia to members that other customers do not get. Clubs can help you distinguish your dispensary and give your customers a sense of belonging.

Offer Deals

You can offer all-day specials or time specific specials to encourage customers to come during off-peak hours. If you have a large morning rush, for example, you can tell customers to come later in the afternoon and receive a discount on rolling papers. You can even offer discounts on holidays. The beauty of a holiday is that you do not have to tell customers that Thanksgiving is coming. April 20, Mother's Day and Black Friday are fast becoming popular days for specials.

Reward with Loyalty Points

Offering electronic or punch card loyalty programs are a great way to build loyal and repeat customers. Seattle Tonics offers a 'fun club' loyalty punch card, for example. Some programs offer points for every dollar spent and bonus points for check-ins for medical marijuana customers, who can receive extra benefits such as a $50 gift voucher, a free hat or T-shirt, and slightly lowered prices on flowers.

Advertise to Reach Customers

Before you advertise, be sure you understand your local laws and are in compliance on the rules of what you can and cannot do.

Focus on your Ideal Customers

By selectively targeting ads to reach your "ideal customer" demographics, you increase your chances of success. For example, if you specialize in edibles and you know some consumers are lactose-intolerant or prefer gluten-free, you might be the only place in town that offers them this treat. The more you connect with your "ideal customer", the more cost effective your choice of advertising will be.

Add a Sense of Urgency

Some ads will bring people into your shop immediately; others plant a seed for future reference. You will attract two types of customers with your ads: those with an ongoing need for your product (e.g. your weekly regulars) and those with a special need (e.g. gifts for Christmas). By adding a sense urgency to your ads, you bring in the first group. The second group will come during those special times.

To add a sense of urgency:

- Always include an end date. For ads in print, the 'special' should end in a week or less. For magazines with a longer shelf life, a 30-day or longer offer is appropriate.

- Include a call to action. Tell them to drop by today, to pick up a loyalty card, to check your website.

- If you have to choose, opt for an ad that will appear more often. Many advertising experts say it takes 3 to 7 times of exposure to an ad before people recognize it and consider making a buy.

You can vary your ads somewhat, but keep them visually consistent and on message.

Show Product Benefits

Sure, you want to say you are "the best cannabis shop in town." But who says? You? If there's no award or recognition, then for most people this sound hollow. Everyone says that. Tell people about what makes you dispensary different from the rest. Your advertising should be about how people will benefit from your products. Many ads list all the features of what the business offers, but a good marketing writer can transform facts into words that give customers reason to buy.

Survey Which Ads are Working

How did customers find you? Did they see the newspaper ad or a YouTube video? Without knowing, it is difficult to eliminate the non-productive advertising from the effective ones. You need to build your marketing in a way that gathers this information.

A few ideas on how to ask customers how they found you:

- Ask customers when taking phone or face-to-face orders.
- Provide a form on the website for customers to fill out.
- Periodically have staff ask customers.
- Include a prepaid postcard survey into their bags.
- Create a comment card to handout that asks the question of how they found you.
- Include a postage-paid reply card in to-go packaging.
- Put codes in coupons indicating when and where they were printed or distributed.
- Use your website's built-in analytics tools to see where traffic is coming from.

To increase response rates, offer discounts or promotional items for the return of the cards. Taking your time to learn which of your ads work best will help you with budgeting decisions on which ads to use.

Promote the Grand Opening

About six to eight weeks before the opening date, contact all of your local suppliers and meet with their sales representatives. They can offer you support, attend, and tell others about your pre-opening launch. Include your shop manager and other key staff to meet with these sales reps, so they can listen and learn from the demonstrations.

Here are a few other tips for the grand opening:

- **Contact the community.** Contact community leaders and residents to come out. Also contact the local media and ask them how much it costs to advertise your first newspaper ad. Opening a new business is a great reason for the local news to feature you.

- **Join the local chamber of commerce or apply to the Better Business Bureau.** Besides lending credibility and establishing yours new business with support, these organizations offer some very good free publicity.

- **Have plenty of brochures on hand.** In this business, information helps people to better understand cannabis. If you are creative, you can design your promotional materials to double as rolling paper filter cutouts or as loyalty buyer cards offering special discounts.

- **Put up your new sign. A** sign is perhaps your best and least expensive promotional tool. As soon as possible, put your sign up (however temporary) to explain the name of the new dispensary, hours of operation and the opening date. People are curious about what is happening in their neighborhood. Give them something to talk about.

Do-It-Yourself Marketing

Many small business owners have advertised and promoted their own businesses without needing any help. While others overspend, fail to increase sales, and never seem to get off the ground. You should do your own marketing if:

- You are interested in learning about marketing.
- You see the big picture while working on the details.
- You have a creative eye.
- This is the best use of your time.

If you have little to no prior experience with marketing, take a look at these resources:

- Learn tips at Leafly.com
- Read *Guerilla Publicity*
- Read *Guerilla Marketing Attack*
- Read *Guerilla Advertising*
- Read *Guerilla Marketing Excellence*
- Read *Guerrilla Social Media Marketing*

Hire Marketing Experts

Hiring an outside advertising firm to do marketing can save you time and money. For fixed-price or hourly rate, a full-service agency could offer:

- **Graphic design to build your image** – provide visual images or design a logo.
- **Marketing campaign** – recommend the right online and offline media to use.
- **Marketing buzz** – start pre-opening 'soft' launch and connect with influencers.
- **Message** – create a sharp slogan that represents your business.
- **Design ads** – produce print, video or web ads.
- **Media buys** – negotiate or purchase time and space for ads.

As a small business, your budget may stop you from hiring a full-service agency, but you can hire a freelance contractor. When hiring a marketing expert, look for:

- Experience in marketing and, if possible, cannabis industry experience.

- Professional approach to business (well-written proposals, contracts).

- Willingness to work within your budget.

Remember, an investment in hiring a marketing expert is an expense that should pay for itself. They help you to create a consistent message, offer you more options than you would otherwise realize by yourself, and steer you away from making otherwise costly mistakes.

Take Action

Marketing involves many steps and lots work to get it right. The following should help you think about your marketing:

- **Study** the laws in your jurisdiction to know what you can and cannot do to promote your dispensary. Recognize the restrictions that apply and keep track of any changes in the law that affects your marketing plans.

- **Ask** for comments. When your dispensary is up and running, tuck a prepaid postcard survey into their shopping bags. Offer discounts or promotional items for the return of the cards. Or have staff hand them out over the counter. If you have emails gathered or a social media community, you can send out online surveys using SurveyMonkey.com to find out what customers think about your dispensary. Ask customers to rate your shop, your products and staff. Ask, "Would you shop here again?" If the answer is "no", find out why and then fix this problem.

- **Review** your "ideal" customer profile. Fine-tune the profiles as you learn more about your customers. When your shop opens, introduce yourself to customers and ask them questions about how they found you and what they think about your products.

- **Promote** your dispensary for the pre-opening launch and put up a sign to inform passersby. Delegate pre-opening tasks to staff to help you set up for launch day.

In today's world, marketing is more than print media and offering promotional brochures, it means having a digital presence. How is your web presence when people search for you on search engines and on various social media platforms?

Chapter 11

Web Presence

" You will undoubtedly face opposition and dissent when you start posting about cannabis online, but you have to be ready to face that and counter it with truth, rather than hide away. You'll never reach influencer status if you've only got one toe dipped in the pool."[170]

RONI STETTER, FOUNDER OF RIGHTEOUS RELATIONS, SAN DIEGO-BASED PUBLIC RELATIONS FIRM

Digital marketing encompasses all web-based communication about your brand to your audience. For cannabis businesses both big and small, digital marketing is appealing because more people are going online than ever before and you can measure the success (or failure) of your digital marketing strategies using key performance metrics like impressions, clicks, and conversion rates. This type of information gives you crucial customer data to determine whether your marketing efforts are paying off or need to be re-thought.

Do I Need a Website?

In a word, "Yes"! It is a crowded market. If you are not visible on people's online searches, for some you do not exist. Your website is your full-colour billboard where you tell people:

- **Who you are** – Cannabis shop extraordinaire.

- **What you make** – We specialize vapes and concentrates.

- **Who you serve** – Serving people in the Waterfront Area since 2017.

- **Where you are located** – At the concern of Main Street and Hillside.

- **When you are open** – Serving people at 7:30 am to 7:00 pm, Monday to Sunday.

- **Why they should buy from you** – We have a selection of locally farmed herb.

- **How to place an order** – Use our online system and your order will be waiting.

Content is King

"Content is King" is an expression used by digital marketers. It means customers pay attention to social media posts and digital content on blogs and websites when it is of value to them. For instance, some people don't know how to roll a joint, while others don't know how to clean their smoking pipes. How do you offer this information?

Show Visuals of Who You Are

Showing pictures of tasty edibles or a cheerful staff always looks good. Remember that your website should reflect your business's personality. If your shop is elegant then you should try to keep a professional appearance and choose colors that show this. If you are playful, then use bolder colors and accents that help to show this feeling. The opportunities are endless. Be imaginative.

Show Videos and Blog

Showing how-to videos can also boost website visitors. You can use the video to explain your product or service in a visual, easy-to-understand way. Blogs provide an opportunity to show your credibility as a dispensary, offering another good way for sharing information in a less formal setting. These videos and blogs link back to your website, which is great for your website's search engine optimization.

Offer Online Menu Choices

This is a good place to show your products and prices. If you have a reputation for selling specialty edibles to "foodies", you can set up an e-commerce website.

Engage Online Visitors

You have many choices. Use both organic and paid social media to drive your audience to your website page. Offer visual or written content that is relevant to your customers' needs, like a blog. You might also create a section for the products you want to promote for the week (the ones you have a surplus of, perhaps, at a good price) and links to Instagram to share photos of your budtenders at work.

Once your business is off the ground, you can upgrade your website to make it interactive with your dispensary's software program, so customers can book appointments and send feedback on what they love about your business.

Send Newsletters to Customers

Create a sign-up section on your homepage and explain how users will benefit from receiving your news and updates. A newsletter is an opportunity for customers to receive news about events and promotions. Having an email-marketing plan will help you build a targeted list that gives you the ability to communicate with customers. Establish a regular monthly cadence with your mailing list so that they do not forget about your business. Just be careful not email them too often – nobody likes a spammer.

Post Events

Announce events on your website that describe what your customers will learn when they visit your store. For instance, you can host events that invites industry authorities like local politicians or business group speakers. Create a calendar of events that will draw people into your store and make them want to keep checking your website. Ideally, your website will bring in business, so it is crucial that you update your website often and respond to feedback in a timely manner. You can also share images, recipes and other content on your social media that would show this and appeal to an online audience.

Digital Marketing

Most of your customers will find you through local advertising, your personal promoting, and word of mouth; but having a web presence does help. Digital marketing can play a vital role. Getting started with establishing your own brand – what makes you different – will be tough. If you are not the only dispensary in your local area, chances are you will need to compete to get customers to your doors.

Design your Websites for Search Engine Optimization

A website is worthless if no one knows it exists. Search engine optimization (SEO) is a critical part of a successful website. Many shoppers use a mobile device when first searching for a dispensary. You will need to think about creating an experience with the mobile visitor in mind. Any time you make the experience easier for a customer, you create a sense of loyalty and they will remember that easy experience next time they consider buying a product with you.

SEO practices are designed to help search engine crawlers to index your website. To take advantage of search traffic, make sure you are targeting the keywords you want your webpages to rank for in areas such as your title tag, meta description, and page copy. Only link to reputable, relevant industry sources to boost your online credibility. For example, if your business is listed on Leafly or Weedmaps, add a link to it on your website so search engine crawlers can factor in reputable, industry relationships into their overall ranking algorithm. Try to update your website often so search engines become accustomed to crawling your website on a regular basis.

Add content to Social Media

With social media, be sure to talk about the products you carry and the ones you are promoting. However, focus on building a rapport more than the products. "Make sure that you follow the guidelines of the platform you're working with so that your account is not suspended or revoked. No consumption. No sales. And whenever possible, keep your content original and don't overly repost," cautions Kristin Ehasz, VP sales at Cannavative, a Nevada-based cultivation and extraction company.[171]

Catherine Goldberg founder of BrainBuzz adds, "Talk directly to your customers with comments, likes, and direct messages to make them feel good and build rapport. Be sure to focus on the experience rather than the product, it has more emotional weight and will increase brand awareness."[172]

The most popular social networks for dispensaries include the following:

Facebook. Facebook is a top-notch social platform for promoting a cannabis dispensary. On average, people spend 40 minutes a day on Facebook, compared to one to three minutes scanning a website.[173] Although people consider Facebook only for personal interactions, it is also useful for businesses. With over one-billion active, one of its biggest age groups is between 45- to 54-year olds.[174] When customers look for local dispensaries on search engines, they will find your Facebook business page, your store's location, hours of operation, images, news updates, articles, and posts that your audience will find valuable.[175]

Twitter. Twitter is proving to be a great platform. Having an active, interesting Twitter account is another way you to reach local customers. In 140 characters or less, you can describe your weekly specials, events or something that will make your customers laugh. Krista Whitley, CEO of Social Media Unicorn, a cannabis marketing and sales agency based in Las Vegas, Nevada, recommends, "since #cannabis and #marijuana are now filtered it is important to capture targeted audiences. Reach out to #wellness, #yoga, #health, and other categories of Twitter users who would be interested in MJ content."[176] You can send tiny URL links about interesting articles, videos, or other content that appeals to your followers, and track the number of clicks received.

Instagram. This platform is image-driven and popular among the cannabis community.[177] "Both the canna-curious and the enthusiasts want to know what happens behind the scenes. Visuals are an opportunity to both redefine the stoner stereotype and share the cultivation and production information that can build brand trust," said Krista Whitley, CEO of Social Media Unicorn.[178] Show beautiful pictures of your products, your business, and any other imagery that reflects your brand and that will resonate with the cannabis community.

Google+. Because Google+ produce unique links back to your website each time you post a message, Google's search engine ranking for your website goes up. Google's social platform is not the most popular, but its benefit in helping your website's search engine optimization is worth paying some attention to.

YouTube. Educational videos will help new users to learn more about cannabis. You might consider creating a few short videos featuring different products and uploading them to your YouTube channel. YouTube might not get immediate results, but few social media platforms have the potential for 'viral-like' videos. If this is an option, you will need to know how to create videos, optimize them for sharing, and how to launch the video. If you do not have the time to create a video, register an account under your brand's name and wait until you are ready.[179] Do not run the risk of losing your brand name on this social media platform. Google owns YouTube. And like Google+, having a YouTube video channel will help you with your website's optimization with every video linked back to your website.

Pinterest. If your brand or products are appealing to women, Pinterest is four times more popular among women than men are.[180] You can create category-specific boards and pin images, products, infographics, recipes, and other content that appeals to the Pinterest audience.[181] According to a study by Converto, in April 2012, Pinterest drove more social media-originated e-commerce sales than Facebook or Twitter.[182] Before 2013, Pinterest only accounted for about 2 percent of global social-mediated sales; however, Pinterest driven ecommerce sales have increased to about 23 percent.[183] Brand studies continued to show Pinterest is more effective at driving sales than other social media.[184]

Vine. Vine is Twitter's new mobile video app launched in January 2013. The main challenge of marketing on Vine is telling or showing an engaging story in six-seconds. You can create a whole series of helpful 'how-to' videos on your Vine account. These short-form video sharing activities are becoming popular with mobile users. If you do not have the time to create videos, open an account under your brand's name and wait until you are ready.

Snapchat. Millennials use Snapchat. Snapchat allows you to send out images and videos to someone before it is deleted. The 'My Story' feature letting users show chronological storylines that are accessible to all of your friends. One way Snapchat has become popular is among fans of celebrities – like Snoop Dog, who promises to have a joint every day. For the cannabis connoisseur who connect with you, receiving a Snapchat from your dispensary about the latest cannabis strains and trends is another way for your regulars to feel plugged in.

Quora and Reddit. Offering thoughtful advice on online community boards like Quora, Reddit, LinkedIn and Facebook is another way to drive traffic to your website. By being selective, you will remain relevant to the discussion and build a reputation. Look for posts related to the cannabis industry and what you do. If you are seen as the expert and offer useful advice, these posts will be seen over and over again – increasing traffic back to your website. At the same time, do not join these forums to sell, people want a discussion in a forum – not a spammy sales pitch.

MassRoots. MassRoots is an up-and-coming social cannabis platform. It is small. As of June 2016, it had an estimated 900,000 users. MassRoots for Business, the company's advertising portal, has an estimated 1,000 clients as of June 2015.

"Make sure you advertise your social media accounts on all of the other ads you put out in magazines, billboards, flyers, etc. Taking all of the regulations surrounding cannabis businesses into account, social media will be your best bet to advertise," said Evan Marder, COO of Matrix NV, Nevada-based cannabis flower and infused products producer.[185]

Email Marketing

Great news for email marketers, cannabis laws permits the sending of "informational promotion or brand-preference promotion to an individual's address". Since customers will opt-in to receive your email newsletters, you have a direct way to connect with a loyal audience. Setting up and managing a weekly or bi-monthly newsletter email marketing campaign is one of the simplest, least expensive, and possibly the most effective tools in your marketing toolkit for building loyal, repeat customers.

Having an email marketing strategy will become even more crucial for building loyal customers as the market becomes saturated. To get subscribers, have a section on your website where people can subscribe. You can have a pop-up with a subscription box and message that explains the newsletter. You should also regularly cross-promote your newsletter on your social media platforms to remind people that it is available.

Your emailed newsletter can include the following:

- New product announcements, discounts or specials (depends on local laws, of course).

- Local in-store or community events that you are involved in or support.

- Informational articles on cannabis culture, local laws, and industry news.

- "Budtender of the Month" or "Shout-Outs to Our Favorite Producers" columns.

- Links to your blog, if you have one (which is recommended).

- Social media links, hours of operation and contact information.[186]

Offering a newsletter is an easy and affordable Do-It-Yourself way for small businesses to market without having to hire an outside agency. Email marketing service companies like MailChimp, Benchmark, and Emma offer different price packages (some even free).

The trick is to offer something enticing that your subscribers want, otherwise they click the "unsubscribe" button or never read what you send. Offering good content helps to build your brand and boosts the chances of being remembered by your subscribers when they want to buy. If this means hiring a marketing copywriter on an ongoing basis, then invest in a good one to help you get your point across more effectively.

Digital Advertising

Google, Facebook and Twitter are not going to let retail dispensaries advertise on their websites. Not yet. According to the Facebook Advertising Guidelines, "Ads may not promote or facilitate the sale or consumption of illegal or recreational drugs, tobacco products, or drug or tobacco paraphernalia."[187] Google Adwords prohibits, "Promotion of substances that alter mental state for the purpose of recreation or otherwise induce 'highs' such as 'marijuana' or 'legal highs'".[188] Twitter has a similar drug policy prohibiting the promotion of 'drugs and drug paraphernalia'.[189] Other major search engines, like Bing and Yahoo, also have strict bans for drug-related advertisements and cites "recreational" drugs as part of the ban.

The good news is that this is changing. Legalization will mean advertising spending – digital and traditional – will grow in this industry. While today's marketers are finding initial stiff resistance, cannabis-friendly advertising platforms are emerging. One digital advertiser stands out: Mantis. Mantis provides ads placed on cannabis-friendly blogs and website. Although Mantis currently only accepts a few businesses for advertising, we may see more companies enter into the marketing to offer these services. WherestheWeed, Leafly and Weedmaps also offer spots for paid advertising.

Do-It-Yourself Websites

You can build a website yourself. You can find free templates online from wix.com and freewebsitetemplates.com. You will need a unique domain name if you want to own your own website – those free templates don't always let you own your own domain or website. Keep in mind the annual renewal costs of the web hosting, domain name registration and continuing need for updating support after the website is done. Every website will eventually need to be updated.

There are also several drawbacks to consider with these do-it-yourself options:

- Some of these templates do not make you look professional.

- Your website needs to work. Broken links and other technical fixes need a real expert.

- They advertise as search-engine and mobile-friendly, but a professional can do better.

- You do not always have the option of owning your website, having to pay monthly.

- Your need a well-written website. A content writer can offer better sales-oriented words.

- Your time invested is better in the hands of someone you hire.

There is always a point of diminishing returns for a Do-It-Yourself developer. You will need to use search engine optimization and take real world actions to promote your website. A well-developed website is an investment in your future – not an expense. Keep your expectations in check for your first website. Invest your time and money wisely.

Hiring Web Pros

Your website is the backbone of every digital marketing campaign you will ever do. While every business owner should at least understand the basics of search engine optimization and website design best practices, establishing a website and digital marketing strategies can feel overwhelming. A professional web developer will help you with these more advanced technical needs. You may want to hire a professional web developer as your business grows.

If you decide to use a professional web developer, you have many choices:

- Search for "web designers" or "digital marketer" in your city or town. One tip is to search for keywords like, "cannabis" and "marijuana" along with "web design" or "marketing" for people in your local area. Look for people with experience in your particular industry.

- Look at other cannabis shop websites. At the bottom of the website, you will often see the company name of the web developer. Take notes of the websites you visit and tell the designer what you like and what you did not.

- Review the developer's portfolio. Does it reflect what you want to see in your website?

Most website developers now double as SEO specialists. Be sure you do your own homework to learn about search engine optimization best practices and in setting realistic goals and expectations for your website.

Take Action

Digital marketing is more than the obvious routes of paid search, email marketing campaigns and social media. Whichever methods you choose, make sure you create a great first impression with an optimized website. The following will help you think about your digital marketing and website needs:

- **Set up** a website with content that engages people to want to read and to come back to your website for updates. This includes setting up an email marketing strategy.

- **Boost** your web presence with search engine optimization that favor marijuana-friendly audiences. This includes creating and managing social media business pages.

- **Recognize** digital advertising restrictions on various social media platforms. You can use advertising available through Leafly, Weedmaps, and WherestheWeed.

- **Promote** your website's domain name at events and on billboards, depending on how your jurisdiction allows you to promote your business.

Web presence will only get you so far. To run a profitable business, you need to consider your sales and costs.

Chapter 12

Managing Sales and Costs

"It's not an exaggeration to say that cannabis businesses face a huge array of challenges that other industries don't even need to consider."[190]

TIM CULLEN, OWNER OF COLORADO HARVEST COMPANY IN DENVER, TAKING ABOUT BANKING AS ONE OF THOSE PROBLEMS

Many people become cost-control converts only after suffering a loss. Make no mistake, high profits can hide inefficiencies. Inefficiencies that you find out about when sales are down. Your main job as a manager is not to put out fires but to prevent them – and to maximize profits in the process. Prevention happens best when you do some advanced planning.

Owning a retail cannabis business requires that you keep track of every item sold or purchased. Your first step is to create systems and procedures for data collection. Understanding this data will lead you to know about your staff's productivity, pricing, marketing effectiveness, and gauging your own competitiveness. Of course, during the first few months, your data will not tell you much; but over time, you will find yourself establishing key benchmarks to measure your performance.

Operations and the Cannabis Laws

In Canada and the eight states that allow recreational cannabis, regulators require all dispensaries to have an inventory tracking system (called a "Marijuana Inventory Tracking System" in Colorado). This system keeps tracks every legally grown plant or cannabis processed product throughout the entire 'seed to sale' cycle.

The system must be able to:

- track cannabis,
- prevent cannabis from being diverted to an illicit market or activity, and
- prevent illicit cannabis from being a source of supply of cannabis in the legal market.

"As more states decriminalize marijuana use, it is imperative that systems be in place to ensure that growers and dispensaries follow proper distribution protocols and comply with state and federal regulations while honoring the ballot measures," said Julie Postlethwait, communications officer with the Colorado's Marijuana Enforcement Division, the Department of Revenue's regulatory agency for the marijuana industry in the state.[191]

Having an inventory tracking system makes sense as a good general business practice and keeps you prepared when your regulator happens to ask you for any inventory information. This also offers you a check and balance system to oversee if theft has occurred. This "seed-to-sale" tracking system is one of the best tools for keeping black market marijuana out of the supply chain.

The Chief Inspector will come to dispensary your without notice and could examine any containers or packages in the shop. They can take photographs and substances to the lab for analysis. The Chief Inspector is authorized to order anyone in the store to identify themselves. The fact is the world is looking at what happens in Canada and the United States with legalized marijuana for recreational use. The result for dispensaries will be stringent enforceable penalties should a problem be found. How you conduct your business and the systems you put in place to monitor your sales, inventories and costs are very important.

Hire a Bookkeeper

Bookkeeping is about counting, analyzing and reconciling all financial transactions. This is a good way to catch sales, inventory and cost control problems. Your in-house bookkeeper's main responsibility is to keep the owners informed about any problem areas by keeping accurate record and balances of all sales, invoices and bills.

Your bookkeeper understands the accounting needs. He or she must understand and appreciate the confidential nature of working for a cannabis business. We recommended the bookkeeper not work in any other capacity, as he or she will be auditing the money and work of the other employees. If you cannot find an in-house bookkeeper, you can hire an outside bookkeeping service.

For most businesses, hiring a skilled part-time bookkeeper to keep track of the financial management of the business is among the wisest decisions you will make for your growing business. For example, getting your employees paid and withholding deposits made accurately and on time can be handled by an in-house bookkeeper with a computerized payroll program and accounting module (such as QuickBooks or Sage 50). If you decide to use an outside payroll or web-based service, your bookkeeper will still be involved in computing the daily labour costs.

Your accountant, on the other hand, works outside of the office, who from time to time will do audits of those records and will be preparing your financial and tax statements. Your accountant will also offer some business advisory services, such as some level of estate planning and Business Planning.

That said, your role as a manager overseeing the financial management cannot be understated. You should spend a couple of hours each day for accounting, regardless of your other commitments. Your involvement in compiling, reporting and analyzing your business's financial data is critical to your dispensary's ability to react to problems.

Meet Your Banker

In Canada, because medical marijuana is legal at the federal level, banks can do business with compliant medical marijuana business owners without being subject to federal penalties. In contract, U.S. a federal prohibition prevents dispensaries from opening business bank accounts, which has forced retail dispensaries to make all transactions in cash – an incentive for criminals on the one hand and a lack of sympathy from law enforcement on the other.

With this in mind, it still is a big deal if you can open a business bank account at all. Canada's banks have closed accounts and turned away prospective account holders that have anything to do with the cannabis industry. Banks are required to monitor businesses for any financial wrongdoing and report suspicious activity to regulators. Under these guidelines, banks must verify that businesses using their services are licensed.

In a statement sent to Cannabis Business Times, AJ Goodman, director of external communications for Royal Bank of Canada, said, "as part of our normal business practices, the bank periodically reviews the client relationships we have against several factors used to balance the benefits and risks associated with providing them with banking services."[192]

In response, Hemp Country owner Nathan MacLellan replied, "Nothing in the store that we sell is illegal. Every single variety store sells pipes and bongs nowadays, so why are they singling us out all of a sudden?"[193]

Choose the Payment Processor

"Consumers spend approximately 25 percent more per transaction when using credit or debit cards," said Vander Veer, recreational shop owner in Colorado.[194] It would seem that having a credit and debit card set up for a dispensary is a must. Not so fast. Your local bank could be able to provide these services, easily, either directly or through a third-party processor. The problem is that by law, banks are constrained by federal laws that make the sale of cannabis illegal.

"Some dispensaries seem to have set up debit card transactions, but they either misled the banks as to the nature of the business or certain companies have discovered creative ways to obtain a merchant account for the dispensaries. Often the result is that once the bank discovers what is happening they close down the account," said CanPay Chief Executive Officer Dustin Eide.[195] Credit card companies like Visa and MasterCard have said they still want nothing to do with selling cannabis products.

To fill this gap, there are cannabis-friendly payment processing companies like Globility Link Inc. or Merrco. There is also CanPay, an app-based payment system that works sort of like PayPal but built for mobile use. Forbes Magazine calls CanPay the "First Legitimate Debit Payment System for Cannabis Purchases."[196]

These payment processing companies must take on a legal and financial compliance role. They will evaluate your finances and legal status for pre-approval, may visit quarterly to make sure your business complying with cannabis law regulations, and follow the funds from seed to sale as required by law. They must comply with the *Bank Secrecy Act* and anti-money laundering compliance, conduct know-your-customer policies and transaction due diligence, and files currency transaction and suspicious activity reports.

At this time, given that most payment processing companies deem the marijuana industry as "high risk", you may not have many choices in choosing your processor. While these services provide convenience in solving a problem, they do not benefit from the deposit insurance and regulatory oversight as do banks. However, as the first-movers into the cannabis industry, these relationships of offering competitive transaction fee may last long after the banking and credit card industries have entered the cannabis industry.

Buy a Point-of-Sale System

MJ Freeway, BioTrackTHC, Cova, and Cannalogic offer cannabis-specific POS systems. Buying a point-of-sale (POS) system is not cheap, but the law requires you have an inventory tracking system. This system must be able to keep track of and hold receipts for all your dispensary's product sales, inventory, and expected taxes.

These intricate systems will alert you whenever inventory levels are off. The touch screen is effortless, requires minimal training and provides extensive sales data. Trying to keep track with QuickBooks is not going to cut it. Do your homework and make sure whatever system you choose will cover all of your state/provincial and federal requirements.

How does it work? Each plant or product has a small tag that allows a scanner gun, similar to that used by a grocery store clerk, to follow the cannabis from "seed to sale".

Julie Weed of Forbes explains that when the plant is divided into bud for smoking, trim for extracts, and waste, each plant receives a unique identification number that relates it to its source. The tracking system carries information from seed through to the final product.

"The software creates an unbroken product lineage. It can forwards-trace a specific plant to every brownie infused with it, and it can backwards-trace a specific brownie to the plant or plants from which its cannabis was derived. The system also then records which licensed dispensary the brownie is shipped to. Regulators will know if a package of marijuana goes missing while in transit. This detailed tracking helps avoid theft during the process and aids product recalls when necessary."[197]

Your POS system can also doubles as a Customer Relationship Management tool, offering email marketing automation and analytics to help you understand your customers. Headset and Baker offer business intelligence reporting systems that you can integrate with most POS systems. You can keep track of your customers' sales data, loyalty program features, and even which budtenders sold which products.

Understand Your Cash Flow

Budgeting is an accounting tool that helps to evaluate how effective the shop's management and employees are at growing sales and controlling expenses during the month. Although your dispensary may only be at the pre-opening stage, now is the time to start to develop your operating budget. Spending four hours each month reviewing your budget is all you need to review this month's budget and prepare a new projected budget for each month. Reviewing this information helps you recognize cost problems and act quickly to correct them. Having a keen sense of the numbers will help you in controlling your costs.

Expect that your Business Plan's first operating budget to be unrealistic. Operating costs will be higher than expected and sales will fluctuate because you have not built a substantial enough loyal customer base. Even with the best-laid plans, assumptions and estimates, it will take a couple of months before you see routine expected and actual operating budgets.

Total Sales

Projecting total sales is the hardest part of budgeting. The fact is, it is almost impossible to know what your sales will be tomorrow, next Wednesday or next month. Estimating your monthly total sales is difficult to do. Most costs are either variable or semi-variable, which means they will fluctuate with your sales projections. Even if your sales projections are not at first accurate, you will be gathering and comparing valuable data – and you will get better at it. After several months of operation, your projections will be right on target.

Discontinue Underperforming Inventory

This is an industry where customers prefer fresh flower. True, cannabis kept out of the light and in airtight containers can be preserved for a very long time. But too long, it begins to lose its terpene smells and potency just like any other spice or herb. For most customers, any cannabis flower sitting on the shelf for more than four or five months is past its prime. Stale flower, edible or any other products gathering dust can take up space. Have too much inventory taking up valuable shelf space, what do you do?

Schedule a pre-shift meeting every day to discuss slow moving products and how the team can sell these products. Reminding your employees about the priorities in managing sales and inventories will help them to self-monitor what they need to do. If your customers show little interest in it, perhaps it is time to discontinue the product.

Lisa Rough of Leafly offers more advice:

Sales, Sales, Sales. Customers often search for deals. This is a great time to pull out the oldest inventory from your shelves. A well-timed, well-planned, and well-promoted sale is a good way to unload extra inventory. Offering the sale as a one-time event makes customers interested in coming back to the shop.

Rearrange your inventory. Customers cannot buy what they cannot see. If you are having trouble moving products, the first step is to make the products more visible. This can mean moving product to a more prominent location, updating your menu to highlight special deals, or creating promotional signage for your display cases.

Bundle your products. If you have tons of one product, offer a special on multiple units of the item. Another way to take advantage of bundling is to pair fast-moving items with less popular items. If, for example, a single infused chocolate bar sells like hotcakes, pairing it with a slower-moving edible at a comparable price makes a sweet deal for an edible-loving cannabis consumer looking to stretch their dollar.

Find creative ways to advertise. You can place flyers, postcards, newspaper inserts, and drink coasters in prominent and popular locations nearby to get the word out about a new deal or promotion. However, pay close attention to your local cannabis advertising guidelines to make sure your advertisements do not break any rules.

Use social media to your advantage. Placing deals and specials on some of your more active social media channels is a way to reward loyalty for your followers. Add a special loyalty rewards code to give a discount to your regular customers and social media followers.[198]

Operating Costs

Customer feedback and sales, affected by seasonal holiday demands and changes in preferences, will affect your choice of products over the next few months. You will have a better idea of what your customers want and are willing to pay. During the

start, allow four to 12 weeks to establish a pattern for your choice of products and for all the bugs to work out in your POS inventory tracking system.

Keep track of the following budgeted expenditures:

- **Supplies/products** such as cannabis, hashish oil, extracts, wax, edibles, water pipes, glass pipes, papers, etc.). These are variable costs.

- **Capital Expenditures** Capital expenditures for equipment, computers and software are depreciated over a set lifespan.

- **Depreciation** is the expense derived from a capital asset's usefulness over the life of the property. Some examples of the depreciable items common in a dispensary include office equipment, building (if owned), and display cases.

- **Payroll.** Manager salary is a fixed monthly cost. Employee salary is a semi-variable cost that fluctuates with the number of employees on the payroll. The wages paid to the bookkeeper are included in the employee labour expenditure.

- **Trade Dues, Business Associations.** This includes dues paid to professional organizations (e.g. Cannabis Friendly Business Association) or business organizations (e.g. Better Business Bureau). Add trade magazine subscriptions in this category.

- **Licenses.** This is the expense of all business and government licenses and permits.

- **Security** is a fixed monthly cost.

- **Legal** is a variable charge that fluctuates.

- **Accounting.** Once you start your business, the accounting expenses should be a monthly charge; except for an annual tax-preparation and year-end audit fee.

- **Maintenance**. Facility maintenance is a fixed monthly expense if you are using a maintenance service company. This includes the cost of minor scheduled repairs, emergency repairs and maintenance to the building. This may also include parking lot cleaning, window cleaning and other cleaning services. Always budget a base amount for normal service. Make adjustments, if you anticipate major repairs.

- **Utilities**. Such as telephone service should be a consistent monthly expense. Electricity may be a semi-variable expense depending on the monthly usage.

- **Rent** is a monthly rent or the monthly lease. Certain business-rental and lease agreements also include a percentage of total sales or pre-tax profit amount. Should this be the case, use the budgeted total sales figure and project the anticipated amount due.

- **Insurance**. Total all insurance premium amounts (fire, theft, liability, workers' compensation, etc.).

- **Advertising**. Advertising includes all the costs of advertising the dispensary, including radio, mailing circulators, newspapers, etc.

- **Promotional Expenses**. This is the expense of promotional items: key chains, calendars, pens, T-shirts, etc.

- **Contributions**. These are all contributions paid to recognized charitable organizations.

- **Property Taxes.** If applicable, divide the annual property tax by 12. This figure will equal the average monthly property tax amount.

- **Payroll Taxes.** This tax is what the employer contributes to the State and federal governments. A separate tax account should be set-up with your bank to keep all the tax money separate. Labour taxes include social security, federal employment insurance and State employment tax.

- **Other Taxes.** This includes all the miscellaneous taxes, such as sales taxes paid on purchases. This column is for any tax the dispensary pays for goods and services.

Control Costs with Audits

Your ability to control costs, overhead, and people has a direct effect on your profits. Cost control is your ability to collect, organize, and compare numbers will affect your bottom line. This is not a job a manager can simply delegate to a bookkeeper or to staff. Managers must be able to work with these sales, inventory and cost numbers to be able to quickly improve anything in your dispensary's cost controls, purchasing procedures or employee's training that is causing discrepancies. Managers must be able to use these numbers to provide owners with valuable decision-making insights that tell the real story of what is going on in your dispensary. These following areas are central to monitor for any cost control and inventory tracking system:

Check Purchases

The goal of purchasing is to find the best products at the lowest possible cost. You will need to have a good working relationship with all of your and vendors and suppliers. This means spending a lot of time meeting with sales representatives and doing research on companies before you decide which products are the best for your dispensary.

Review Receiving

Receiving is where you verify that everything you ordered has arrived. When a product arrives, check for the correct brands, grades, varieties, quantities, and correct prices before sending them to storage. Check products purchased by count or weight, if possible.

Count Inventory Levels

You will need to know when scheduled deliveries arrive and the amounts used in the period. Begin tracking inventory levels by setting up a buying schedule, using a calendar posted on the office wall that shows:

- Contact information for customer service and/or sales reps for each vendor.

- What items will be arriving from which company?

- Which day's orders need to be placed?

- When deliveries will be arriving?

- The price the sales representative quoted or other special pricing/discounts.[199]

This tells you what inventory you brought in, what day, and how much. You need to keep precise information about what is coming into your store – and going out. When a delivery does not arrive as scheduled, you must call the company immediately. Do not wait a day.

To have control over inventory, you need to find your store's minimum and maximum inventory needs. If you know your minimum level, you will know when to reorder before running out.

But you can only really do reorder when you know how much you need and how much you actually have on hand. And you can only really know how much you have on hand when you have a physical inventory count.

You might be tempted to rely on your computerized **POS** inventory tracking system to alert you when to purchase, but there is nothing more thorough in finding errors and problems in procedures than an actual inventory count. You should do an inventory count at least every three months. Knowing your daily, weekly or monthly consumption by customers and the exact planned delivery times will keep you on top of having the proper quantities on hand.

At the beginning, it is a good idea to count physical inventory every week to ensure the accuracy and trustworthiness of your staff in following inventory storage procedures. Conducting this routine audit exercise will train you to have an almost intuitive sense of how much your regular orders should contain.

Review Order Taking

Every item sold or issued needs to be recorded by computer, cash register or manually. It needs to be impossible for anyone to get products without having them entered into the system.

Review Cash Receipts

Monitoring sales is crucial to cost controls. Under/over-charging and lost paperwork must be investigated daily. Compile all of your sales information to build a historical financial record. This record will help you with forecasting future sales.

Reconcile Bank Deposits / Accounts Payable

Conduct a review of bank deposits and charge slips.

Cost control is an ongoing process that involves every employee. Setting easy-to-follow systems and procedures will make your data more accurate. A continual review of this cost control process is integral to the functioning of your dispensary.

Take Action

Managing sales and costs through an accounting and inventory tracking system takes time, but must be done daily. The following will help you prepare your sales and cost systems:

- **Set up** an inventory tracking system. Talk to your banker, bookkeeper, and payment processor, along with the POS system vendor, to establish best practices.

- **Prepare** a budget to help keep track of actual and expected sales and operating costs.

- **Track** sales with a focus on choosing the right product mix. Discontinue poor performing inventory and make plans to sell off remaining slow moving products.

- **Focus** on cost controls and monitoring of expenses with the help of internal audits and established procedures for routine checks on your inventory and costs.

You will need to think about how your business will grow. For this, you need to think about an Exit Plan.

Chapter 13

The Exit Plan

"Any would-be cannabis entrepreneur should be aware of the fact that the cannabis space is one of the riskier and more complicated industries to get involved in, whether they plan on touching the plant or pursuing ancillary business models. There exist many more industries that might serve as easier spaces for entrepreneurs to get started in, but the cannabis space has boundless potential and is a great deal of fun. I suspect those factors are the main ones that continue to draw in enthusiasts from all walks of life."[200]

RICHARD HUANG, CEO OF CLOUDIOUS9, A HIGH-TECH VAPORIZER COMPANY BASED IN SILICON VALLEY

It may seem odd at the start of a business to develop an Exit Plan. If you have potential investors or lenders, they definitely want to know your long-term plans. Rarely do new cannabis business owners start businesses with this in mind. But let's be honest, no one can predict what life event will cause you to leave. Maybe a sudden need to move to another city for a loved one, early retirement because of a health problem or some other big challenge. There are no crystal balls here.

That is why the best time to prepare for the future is now, at the beginning. If you can think ahead, then maybe you have a better chance of selling your business at a higher price. After all, your dispensary is supposed to be your ticket to a healthy nest egg.

Your Business (Exit) Plan

Just as you are writing your first Business Plan, include a short section for your Exit Plan. When it comes to Exit Plan, you only have two options:

- **Sell your share:** Sell your equity to the existing partners or someone who wants to buy your share. The sales price is based on the estimate of future sales (often the last three to five years of sales trends).

- **Liquidate:** Sell all of your assets at market value and use the money to pay off any remaining debts. This is a simple approach but also the least profitable.

A good Business Plan will outline your most likely exit strategy from day one. Your Exit Plan should cover:

- **Your best-case scenario.** When do you want to retire? Will your family continue running the dispensary? Do you want the business to be sold?

- **Your worst-case scenario.** What will happen in an emergency? Do you have a will?

- **Ways to improve the business's value.** Can you increase sales or profits? What changes you can make that will make your business more attractive to a buyer? Have you developed a succession plan of who will replace you?

- **Your current value.** How much could you get in cash if you liquidated it today? What are the tax implications? Hiring a business evaluator and accountant will help answer these questions. Calculating a business's value involves making estimates of the potential future earnings of your business and assessing a reasonable fair market price.

Your lawyer and accountant can help you with advisory services to create your Exit Plan. Remember to review and update your Exit Plan (and Business Plan) annually.

Finding Your Replacement

Be careful about who you sell to before you decide to sell the business. Someone who just wants to make a few extra bucks could cheapen all your hard work. A natural part of finding a replacement is envisioning whether this other person would be a good successor. How would the new buyer treat your employees? The customers? The choice of new products and vendors? Grooming a replacement will take time, especially if you continue to remain financially tied to the success of the dispensary after the sale.

A successor will bring his or her own talents, desires, and limitations. This is not a time for you to create a clone of yourself. If you have a candidate in mind, start by sharing your vision of the future you see. Work together to develop a plan, and listen to his or her ideas and needs. This is your time to examine and improve "problems" before the sale. When you find your replacement, share what you know and what you think needs to be done to move the dispensary forward.

Talk to the Professionals

Many businesses are family operated. The success of your Exit Plan will depend on how well prepared you are at transferring your dispensary's assets. You want to minimize the tax burden on the next generation or to someone else outside the family.

Preparing the inheritance tax paperwork, trust or tax-free gifts are all complicated to do and are best left to professionals – which sometimes can take up to 10 years to resolve. You will need to meet with estate planners, accountants and lawyers to ensure this is a smooth transition.

Selling to Employees

If your dispensary is profitable and you have at least 10 to 15 employees, then setting up an Employee Owned Stock Plans (ESOP) deserve a closer look. Funding for this option comes from the tax-deductible future earnings of the dispensary, not from employees' paychecks. The ESOP option allows employees to buy your business as they would if they were any other potential buyer. Taking this step will require finding a lawyer who knows how to draft an ESOP plan.

There are also several risks with this option. One risk is that unless the former employees have enough capital saved up in the ESOP, you might have to underwrite some of the financing with a bank. Banks will work with ESOP loans as other loans, but they will look payrolls in relation to the cash flow and collateral of the business to service the debt.[201]

Friendships can also feel strained when it comes time to haggle over the final price. In some cases, owners may feel hurt when employees want to change something to the store the owner wants to keep. This is a good time for the lawyer or accountant to act as a go-between and to keep the selling process professional and less emotionally charged.

Take Action

The more you work on your Business Plan, the more the Exit Plan become a driving force in helping you to shape your future. The following will help you think about the Exit Plan:

- **Write** your Exit Plan to discuss the options and your best- and worst-case scenarios that could present obstacles and opportunities for you in reaching your long-term goals.

- **Find** a replacement for yourself with someone who carries the same vision as you. This person does not have to be exactly like you. You will need to be open to changes that respect the other person's talents and interests.

- **Hire** professionals like bankers, accountants, estate planners and lawyers to help you oversee your Exit Plan and transition plans for leaving the business. A professional business evaluator will also need to be hired to assess market value.

- **Consider** selling your business to employees by setting up an ESOP. This is like any other sale but may require personal considerations since the buyer worked for you.

Continue to come back to your Business Plan every three or four months (no longer than once a year). You will tweak parts and update others.

May the knowledge imparted to you through this book continue to help you grow.

Resources

The author makes no endorsement of the links ᴅ₋
links were selected because they appeared as cannabis-ᴛʜₑ
organizations. Not an endorsement. Retail focused.

Both Canada and United States

Advertising

- Leafly

- Mantis

- Weedmaps

- WherestheWeed

Associations and Organizations

- International Cannabis Association

Business Advice

- Dispensary Management Today

- Gangapreneur.com –
  www.ganjapreneur.com/topic/advice

- Leafly.com – www.leafly.com/news/industry

...siness Intelligence – Analytics

- Baker – http://trybaker.com

- Headset IO - http://headset.io

Conferences

- International Cannabis Business Conference

Point of Sales

- BioTrackTHC – www.biotrack.com/dispensary-point-of-sale

- Cova – www.covasoft.com/

- MJ Freeway – https://mjfreeway.com/geo/ca

Publications

- 420intel.com – http://420intel.com/regional/canada

- Cannabis Business Times – www.cannabisbusinesstimes.com

- Cannabis Industry Journal – www.cannabisindustryjournal.com

- Cannabis Life Network – https://cannabislifenetwork.com

- Marijuana News – www.marijuana.com/news

- Marijuana Business Magazine – https://mjbizmagazine.com

- High Times - http://hightimes.com/

Training

- Cannabis College – www.cannabiscollege.com

- Cannabis Training Institute – https://cannabistraininginstitute.com

- Cannabis Training University – https://cannabistraininguniversity.com

- Oaksterdam University – http://oaksterdamuniversity.com

- THC University – www.thcuniversity.org

- *The Official High Times Field Guide to Marijuana Strains,* by Danny Danko

Canada

Accounting and Financial

- Hutcheson and Co. LLP – www.hutcheson.ca/about-us/philip-hogan

- MNP LLP – www.mnp.ca

Associations and Organizations

- Canadian Association of Medical Cannabis Dispensaries

- Cannabis Canada

- Cannabis Growers of Canada

- Cannabis Friendly Business Association

- Cannabis Patients Association of Canada

- National Institute for Cannabis Health and Educations

- The Cannabis Trade Alliance of Canada

Conferences

- Cannabis Life Conference

- Canadian Cannabis Business Conference

- Lift Cannabis Business Conference

- O'Cannabiz Conference & Expo

Dispensary Design

- figure3

Employees

- Unifor

Law

- *Cannabis Act* – www.parl.ca/DocumentViewer/en/42-1/bill/C-45/first-reading

- Marijuana Laws – www.marijuanalaws.ca

Legal

- Aird & Berlis

- LaBarge Weinstein LLP – www.lwlaw.com/people/weinstein-deborah

- Minden Gross LLP

Municipalities

- City of Vancouver – http://vancouver.ca/doing-business/medical-marjiuana-related-business-regulations.aspx

- City of Victoria – www.victoria.ca/en/main/business/permits-licenses/medical-cannabis-businesses.html

Payment Processing

- Globility Link Inc

- Merrco

Point of Sales

- Cannalogic

- Viridian Sciences

Security

- Securifort-Gardex

- Tri West Technologies

Publications

- Cannabis Life Network

- Lift News

- Skunk Magazine

United States – Laws

For legal recreational states only.

Advertising Rules

- Alaska - *Chapter 306. Regulation of the Marijuana Industry*

- California - *Chapter 15. Advertising and Marketing Restrictions*

  - Colorado - *Colorado Retail Marijuana Regulations*

  - Massachusetts - *Implementation of an Act for the Humanitarian Medical Use of Marijuana*

  - Nevada - *Advertising Guidelines for Medical Marijuana Establishments (MMEs)*

  - Oregon - *Oregon's Medical Marijuana Dispensary Program Forms and Signage*

  - Washington - *Washington State Legislature section on cannabis advertising*

Associations and Organizations

- National Cannabis Industry Association

Employees

- Colorado's Guide for Marijuana Occupational Safety and Health – https://Colorado.gov/pacific/cdphe/marijuana-occupational-safety-and-health

Laws - General

- Cannabis Law Blog - http://www.cannalawblog.com/

Laws - Alaska

- *An Act to tax and regulate the production, sale and use of marijuana*

- *Draft Regulations for Onsite Consumption*

Laws - California

- *Senate Bill 420*

- *Health and Safety Code Section 11357-11362.9*

- *Proposition 64*

Laws - Colorado

- *Colorado's Laws about Marijuana Use*

- *Retail Marijuana Use in the City of Denver*

- *Colorado Marijuana and Medical Marijuana Statutes*

Laws - Maine

- *Rules Governing the Maine Medical Use of Marijuana Program*

- *Title 22: Health and Welfare, Chapter 262-263*

Laws - Massachusetts

- *Public Consumption of Marihuana or Tetrahydrocannabinol*

Laws - Nevada

- *Chapter 453A – Medical Use of Marijuana*

- *General Provisions of the Uniform Controlled Substances Act*

Laws - Oregon

- *Chapter 475B – Cannabis Regulation*

- *Chapter 153 – Violations and Fines*

Washington

- *Title 7, Chapter 7.80, Section 7.80.120 of the Revised Code Washington.*

- *Title 70, Chapter 70.10, Section 70.160.070 of the Revised Code Washington*

Starting a Marijuana Business

- Smart Biz Trends - https://smallbiztrends.com/2017/01/marijuana-business-laws-by-state.html

Endnotes

1 Jeremiah Wilhelm, "Understanding Medical vs. Adult-Use Cannabis Dispensaries", https://www.leafly.com/news/cannabis-101/what-is-a-marijuana-dispensary (Leafly: read July 2017).

2 Julie Weed. "Cannabis CEOs Advise Aspiring Weed Entrepreneurs on Rules, Risks and Capital Needs," https://www.forbes.com/sites/julieweed/2017/04/10/cannabis-ceos-advise-would-be-weed-entrepreneurs-on-evaluating-rules-risks-and-capital-needs/#4e8085c395b3 (Forbes: 10 April 2017).

3 Paul Chaney, "Starting a Marijuana Business: A State by State Guide", https://smallbiztrends.com/2017/01/marijuana-business-laws-by-state.html (Small Business Trends: January 2017).

4 Medical Marijuana Inc., "1in 5 Medical Marijuana Users Live in States where it's Not Legal, Study Finds", http://www.medicalmarijuanainc.com/1-5-medical-marijuana-users-live-states-not-legal-study-finds (30 December 2016).

5 Patrick Cain, "Canada will see 900,000 new pot smokers under legalization, poll implies", http://globalnews.ca/news/2995390/canada-will-see-900000-new-pot-smokers-under-legalization-poll-implies/ (Global News, Toronto, a division of Corus Entertainment Inc.: 12 October 2016).

6 Lauren Sherman. "Is Marijuana the Luxury Industry's Next Big Opportunity?", https://www.businessoffashion.com/articles/intelligence/is-marijuana-the-luxury-industrys-next-big-opportunity (Business of Fashion: 5 January 2017).

7 Marijuana Business Daily, "Marijuana Business Factbook 2016" (2016). p. 10.

8 Melia Robinson, "The legal weed market is growing as fast as broadband internet in the 2000s", http://www.businessinsider.com/arcview-north-america-marijuana-industry-revenue-2016-2017-1?op=1 (Business Insider:

3 January 2017).

9 Deloitte Canada partnered with RIWI, "Recreational Marijuana: Insights and opportunities" (Toronto: 2016), p 5.

10 Melia Robinson, "The legal weed market is growing as fast as broadband internet in the 2000s", http://www.businessinsider.com/arcview-north-america-marijuana-industry-revenue-2016-2017-1?op=1 (Business Insider: 3 January 2017).

11 Randi Druzin, "The Ontario Proposition: Details and Feedback from the Scene", https://www.leafly.com/news/politics/the-ontario-proposition-details-and-feedback-from-the-scene (Leafly: 8 September 2017).

12 Arvind Dilawar, "Pot blocks: obstacles keep small business owners from a multibillion-dollar market," https://www.theguardian.com/society/2016/dec/31/legal-marijuana-pot-cannabis-dispensary-small-business-regulation (The Guardian: 31 December 2016).

13 The Canadian Press. "Real money is in recreational marijuana': Businesses look forward to a pivotal 2017", https://news.lift.co/an-interview-with-david-hyde-on-the-future-of-commercial-cannabis-production-in-Canada/ (Financial Post, Toronto, 23 December 2016).

14 Medical Marijuana Inc., "1in 5 Medical Marijuana Users Live in States where it's Not Legal, Study Finds", http://www.medicalmarijuanainc.com/1-5-medical-marijuana-users-live-states-not-legal-study-finds (30 December 2016).

15 Office of the Parliamentary Budget Officer, "Legalized Cannabis: Fiscal Considerations" (Ottawa, Parliamentary Budget Office, 2016), p. 4.

16 Randi Druzin, "The Ontario Proposition: Details and Feedback from the Scene", https://www.leafly.com/news/politics/the-ontario-proposition-details-and-feedback-from-the-scene (Leafly: 8 September 2017).

17 Patrick Cain, "How will legal pot be sold? Three things that might happen, and one that won't", https://globalnews.ca/news/2987372/how-will-legal-pot-be-sold-liquor-stores-are-most-likely-option/ (Global News: 9 October 2016).

18 Las Vegas, Nevada government website, "Marijuana Licenses", https://lasvegasnevada.gov/portal/faces/wcnav_externalId/bl-med-

marijuana?_adf.ctrl-state=djj7p1_4&_afrLoop=3328562998937136&_afrWindowMode=0&_afrWindowId=null#%40%3F_afrWindowId%3Dnull%26_afrLoop%3D3328562998937136%26_afrWindowMode%3D0%26_adf.ctrl-state%3Do502b4cye_4 (Las Vegas, Nevada government website: read on August 2017).

[19] Sunny Freeman, "Half of Canadian pot smokers surveyed spend on average $100 on weekly buzz: report", http://business.financialpost.com/commodities/agriculture/half-of-canadian-pot-smokers-surveyed-spend-100-on-weekly-buzz-report/wcm/08e02deb-ec02-4dc7-bc84-ac3f48d674ef (Financial Post: 14 December 2016).

[20] Debra Borchardt, "Cannabis Shoppers Come For One Thing, But Leave With Impulse Buys", https://www.forbes.com/sites/debraborchardt/2017/03/03/cannabis-shoppers-come-for-one-thing-but-leave-with-impulse-buys/#56519cb67b91 (Forbes: 3 March 2017).

[21] Alastair Sharp, "Canada's top marijuana producer to double production", https://www.reuters.com/article/us-canopy-growth-cannabis/canadas-top-marijuana-producer-to-double-production-idUSKCN1BI2Y1 (Reuters: 7 September 2017).

[22] Ibid.

[23] Ibid.

[24] Matt Lamers, "Legal, regulatory obstacles preventing Canadian 'Big Cannabis' from diving headfirst into U.S", https://mjbizdaily.com/canadas-big-cannabis-mostly-avoiding-us-market-owing-potential-pitfalls/ (Marijuana Business Daily: 10 August 2017).

[25] James McClure, "This Is How Olympic Snowboarder Ross Rebagliati Thinks Pot Shops Should Work", https://www.civilized.life/articles/ross-rebagliati-pot-shops/ (Civilized: 23 August 2017).

[26] Ibid.

[27] Laura Kane, "'Craft cannabis' growers fight for legal role", http://www.timescolonist.com/life/islander/craft-cannabis-growers-fight-for-

legal-role-1.2287891 (The Canadian Press: 26 June 2016).

28 Sunny Freeman, "Half of Canadian pot smokers surveyed spend on
   average $100 on weekly buzz: report",
   http://business.financialpost.com/commodities/agriculture/half-of-canadian-
   pot-smokers-surveyed-spend-100-on-weekly-buzz-report/wcm/08e02deb-
   ec02-4dc7-bc84-ac3f48d674ef (Financial Post: 14 December 2016).

29 David Brown., "The future of commercial cannabis production in Canada",
   https://news.lift.co/an-interview-with-david-hyde-on-the-future-of-
   commercial-cannabis-production-in- Canada / (Life News, Toronto: 9
   March 2017)

30 Matt Lamers, "Legal, regulatory obstacles preventing Canadian 'Big
   Cannabis' from diving headfirst into U.S", https://mjbizdaily.com/canadas-
   big-cannabis-mostly-avoiding-us-market-owing-potential-pitfalls/ (Marijuana
   Business Daily: 10 August 2017).

31 Jeremy White, "California is about to open its first legal cannabis shops and
   it's posing a huge problem for local pot farms",
   http://www.independent.co.uk/news/world/americas/california-cannabis-
   legal-weed-marijuana-farms-supply-demand-issues-a7931146.html
   (Independent: 5 September 2017).

32 Ibid.

33 Thomas Fuller, "Legal Marijuana Is Almost Here. If Only Pot Farmers Were
   on Board", https://www.nytimes.com/2017/09/09/us/california-marijuana-
   growers.html (The New York Times: 9 September 2017).

34 Thomas Fuller, "Legal Marijuana Is Almost Here. If Only Pot Farmers Were
   on Board", https://www.nytimes.com/2017/09/09/us/california-marijuana-
   growers.html (The New York Times: 9 September 2017).

35 Chris Roberts, "California Has a Dirty Cannabis Problem",
   https://www.leafly.com/news/politics/leafly-investigation-california-dirty-
   cannabis-problem (Leafly: 15 February 2017).

36 Addison Herron-Wheeler, "Concentrate vs. Flower",
   http://ireadculture.com/concentrate-vs-flower/ (Culture Magazine: 7 July
   2016).

37 Grant Robertson, "Pesticide-laden medical marijuana spurs third Canadian
   lawsuit", https://www.theglobeandmail.com/news/national/pesticide-laden-

medical-marijuana-spurs-third-lawsuit/article34308153/ (The Globe and Mail, Toronto: 14 March 2017).

[38] Debra Borchardt, "Cannabis Lab Testing Is the Industry's Dirty Little Secret", https://www.forbes.com/sites/debraborchardt/2017/04/05/cannabis-lab-testing-is-the-industrys-dirty-little-secret/#1dba40801220 (Forbes: 5 April 2017).

[39] Ibid.

[40] Ibid.

[41] Solomon Israel, "Aurora Cannabis to disclose marijuana testing data to ease public concerns", http://www.cbc.ca/news/business/aurora-cannabis-marijuana-testing-1.4017043 (CBC News, Toronto: 9 March 2017).

[42] MMD Insurance, "MMD Offers Product Liability Coverage for Medical Cannabis Firms", http://www.insurancejournal.com/news/national/2010/11/01/114512.htm (Insurance Journal: 1 November 2010).

[43] Julie Weed, "Cannabis CEOs Advise Aspiring Weed Entrepreneurs on Rules, Risks and Capital Needs," https://www.forbes.com/sites/julieweed/2017/04/10/cannabis-ceos-advise-would-be-weed-entrepreneurs-on-evaluating-rules-risks-and-capital-needs/#4e8085c395b3 (Forbes: 10 April 2017).

[44] Matt Guerry and Caralyn Reese, "Permits to be issued soon for Pa. medical marijuana facilities", http://www.centredaily.com/news/local/article149413829.html. (Centre Daily Times: 8 May 2017).

[45] Arvind Dilawar, "Pot blocks: obstacles keep small business owners from a multibillion-dollar market," https://www.theguardian.com/society/2016/dec/31/legal-marijuana-pot-cannabis-dispensary-small-business-regulation (The Guardian: 31 December 2016).

[46] WikiHow, "How to Put up a Medical Dispensary", http://www.wikihow.com/Put-up-a-Medical-Marijuana-Dispensary

(WikiHow: retrieved July 2017).

[47] Jeff Grissler, Marijuana Business (2015), p.28.

[48] Arvind Dilawar, "Pot blocks: obstacles keep small business owners from a multibillion-dollar market," https://www.theguardian.com/society/2016/dec/31/legal-marijuana-pot-cannabis-dispensary-small-business-regulation (The Guardian: 31 December 2016).

[49] Michael Roberts, "Marijuana business failure rate of 40 percent not bad, says industry expert", http://www.westword.com/news/marijuana-business-failure-rate-of-40-percent-not-bad-says-industry-expert-5830875 (Westword: 7 March 2017).

[50] Sharon Fuller and Douglas Brown, How to Open a Financially Successful Bakery (Atlantic Publishing Group, Florida: 2004) p. 29.

[51] Votleface, "The Rise of the Cannabis Connoisseur", http://volteface.me/features/rise-cannabis-connoisseur (Volteface: read on August 2017).

[52] Canopy Growth Corporation, "Medical marijuana producer supports MADD Canada", http://mytoba.ca/news/medical-marijuana-producer-supports-madd-canada (MyToba: 16 May 2016).

[53] Rob Ferguson, "Ontario prepping reefer awareness campaign on the dangers of marijuana as legalization date approaches", https://www.thestar.com/news/queenspark/2017/07/28/ontario-prepping-reefer-awareness-campaign-on-the-dangers-of-marijuana-as-legalization-date-approaches.html (The Star: 28 July 2017).

[54] Debra Borchardt, "The Average Cannabis Customer Spends $600 A Year", https://www.civilized.life/articles/the-average-cannabis-customer-spends-600-a-year/ (Civilized Life: 12 May 2017).

[55] Shan Li, "Marijuana shops are trying to look like the Apple store", http://www.latimes.com/business/la-fi-fancy-pot-shops-20161230-story.html (Los Angeles Times: 16 Jan 2017).

[56] Ibid.

[57] Winnie Hu, "When Retirement Comes with a Daily Dose of Cannabis", https://www.nytimes.com/2017/02/19/nyregion/retirement-medicinal-

marijuana.html (The New York Times: 19 February 2017).

58 Ibid.

59 Robert Celt, "Mom and Dad Make Up 45% Of Medical Marijuana Patients", https://www.420magazine.com/2016/02/mom-and-dad-make-up-45-of-medical-marijuana-patients (420 Magazine: 29 February 2017).

60 Ibid.

61 Lift News, "Patient Voices: An Interview with a Medical Marijuana Patient", https://news.lift.co/patient-voices-an-interview-with-a-medical-marijuana-patient/Life (Lift News: 10 August 2015).

62 Winnie Hu, "When Retirement Comes with a Daily Dose of Cannabis", https://www.nytimes.com/2017/02/19/nyregion/retirement-medicinal-marijuana.html (The New York Times: 19 February 2017).

63 Shan Li, "Marijuana shops are trying to look like the Apple store", http://www.latimes.com/business/la-fi-fancy-pot-shops-20161230-story.html (Los Angeles Times: 16 Jan 2017).

64 Miner & Co Studio, "The New Cannabis Consumer- Stoners No More", http://www.minerandcostudio.com/a-new-class-of-cannabis-consumers (Miner & Co Studio: 30 November 2017).

65 Debra Borchardt, "The Average Cannabis Customer Spends $600 A Year", https://www.civilized.life/articles/the-average-cannabis-customer-spends-600-a-year/ (Civilized Life: 12 May 2017).

66 Julie Weed, "How Entrepreneurs Are Helping Consumers Enjoy Cannabis Discreetly," https://www.forbes.com/sites/julieweed/2017/02/07/entrepreneurs-help-consumers-enjoy-cannabis-discreetly/#51219d42356e (Forbes: 7 February 2017).

67 Office of the Parliamentary Budget Officer. Legalized Cannabis: Fiscal Considerations. (Ottawa, Parliamentary Budget Office, 2016), p. 2.

68 Sunny Freeman, "Half of Canadian pot smokers surveyed spend on average $100 on weekly buzz: report",

http://business.financialpost.com/commodities/agriculture/half-of-canadian-pot-smokers-surveyed-spend-100-on-weekly-buzz-report/wcm/08e02deb-ec02-4dc7-bc84-ac3f48d674ef (Financial Post: 14 December 2016).

[69] Debra Borchardt, "The Average Cannabis Customer Spends $600 A Year", https://www.civilized.life/articles/the-average-cannabis-customer-spends-600-a-year/ (Civilized Life: 12 May 2017).

[70] Ibid.

[71] Ibid.

[72] Shan Li, "Marijuana shops are trying to look like the Apple store", http://www.latimes.com/business/la-fi-fancy-pot-shops-20161230-story.html (Los Angeles Times: 16 Jan 2017).

[73] Ibid.

[74] Jason Gray, "Cannabis connoisseurs: New market emerging to help educate buyers", http://www.thecannabist.co/2014/05/12/cannabis-connoisseurs/11185 (The Cannabist: 12 May 2014).

[75] Ibid.

[76] The Stranger, "The Stranger's Guide to Every Recreational Weed Store in Seattle", http://www.thestranger.com/weed/2016/11/16/24677904/the-strangers-guide-to-every-recreational-weed-store-in-seattle (The Stranger: 16 November 2016).

[77] Richardo Baca, "You'll be surprised at how shockingly little Willie Nelson knows about weed", http://www.thecannabist.co/2015/11/02/willie-nelson-weed-marijuana/43139/ (The Cannabist: 2 November 2015).

[78] Ibid.

[79] Bailey Rahn, "How to Help Your Friends Who Are Smoking Cannabis for the First Time", https://www.leafly.com/news/cannabis-101/how-to-help-friends-smoking-cannabis-for-the-first-time (Leafly: read August 2017).

[80] Bailey Rahn, "Cannabis Strain Recommendations for Beginners and Low-Tolerance Consumers", https://www.leafly.com/news/strains-products/cannabis-strains-for-beginners-and-lightweights (Leafly: read August 2017).

81 Patrick Bennett, "How to Find the Best Cannabis Experience and High for You", https://www.leafly.com/news/cannabis-101/how-to-find-best-cannabis-experience-high (Leafly: read August 2017).

82 Bailey Rahn, "Cannabis Strain Recommendations for Beginners and Low-Tolerance Consumers", https://www.leafly.com/news/strains-products/cannabis-strains-for-beginners-and-lightweights (Leafly: read August 2017).

83 Patrick Bennett, "How to Find the Best Cannabis Experience and High for You", https://www.leafly.com/news/cannabis-101/how-to-find-best-cannabis-experience-high (Leafly: read August 2017).

84 Diana Budds, "UX Is Changing How We Get High", https://www.fastcodesign.com/3065997/ux-is-changing-how-we-get-high (Co.Design: 1 Dec 2016).

85 Ibid.

86 Ibid.

87 Adrian Sedlin, "Here's what makes our marijuana 'top shelf' – and worth a 25% premium", https://www.cnbc.com/2017/08/08/what-makes-our-luxury-marijuana-worth-25-percent-more-ceo-commentary.html (CNBC: 8 August 2017).

88 Ibid.

89 The Stranger, "The Stranger's Guide to Every Recreational Weed Store in Seattle", http://www.thestranger.com/weed/2016/11/16/24677904/the-strangers-guide-to-every-recreational-weed-store-in-seattle (The Stranger: 16 November 2016).

90 Dana Dovey, "Is Marijuana Addiction Real? Study Finds Habitual Pot Smokers Show Signs of Dependence and Withdrawal", http://www.medicaldaily.com/marijuana-addiction-real-study-finds-habitual-pot-smokers-show-signs-dependence-and-301362 (Medical Daily: 4 September 2014).

91 Ibid.

[92] Julie Weed, "Cannabis Companies Find More Customers That Want Less THC," https://www.forbes.com/sites/julieweed/2017/04/17/cannabis-companies-embrace-micro-dosing-to-broaden-customer-base/#27697252bfe7 (Forbes: 17 April 2017).

[93] James McClure, "Olympian Ross Rebagliati: 'The Idea That There's A Difference Between Medical And Recreational Pot Is Bullshit'", https://www.civilized.life/articles/ross-rebagliati-difference-between-medical-and-recreational-pot/ (Civilized: 1 September 2017).

[94] Dante Jordan, "How to Prepare for a Cannabis Tolerance Break", https://www.leafly.com/news/cannabis-101/how-to-prepare-for-a-cannabis-tolerance-break (Leafly: read August 2017).

[95] The Stranger, "The Stranger's Guide to Every Recreational Weed Store in Seattle", http://www.thestranger.com/weed/2016/11/16/24677904/the-strangers-guide-to-every-recreational-weed-store-in-seattle (The Stranger: 16 November 2016).

[96] Andrea Rowland, "10 tips for choosing the perfect domain name", https://www.godaddy.com/garage/smallbusiness/launch/10-tips-for-choosing-the-perfect-domain-name/ (Godaddy.com: 16 September 2015).

[97] The Stranger, "The Stranger's Guide to Every Recreational Weed Store in Seattle", http://www.thestranger.com/weed/2016/11/16/24677904/the-strangers-guide-to-every-recreational-weed-store-in-seattle (The Stranger: 16 November 2016).

[98] Ibid.

[99] Ibid.

[100] Ibid.

[101] Debra Borchardt, "Cannabis Shoppers Come for One Thing, But Leave with Impulse Buys", https://www.forbes.com/sites/debraborchardt/2017/03/03/cannabis-shoppers-come-for-one-thing-but-leave-with-impulse-buys/2/#73bfc055fa67 (Forbes: 3 March 2017).

[102] Ibid.

[103] Jacquie Miller, "National Cannabis Region: Illegal pot stores pop up across

Ottawa", http://ottawacitizen.com/news/local-news/marijuana-dispensary-chains-move-into-ottawa-as-illegal-pot-stores-pop-up-across-town (Ottawa Citizen, Ottawa: 7 July 2016).

[104] Douglas Brown, "Spotlight: The State of Concentrates", http://www.cannabisbusinesstimes.com/article/spotlight-the-state-of-concentrates (Cannabis Business Times: 29 July 2017).

[105] Jacquie Miller, "National Cannabis Region: Illegal pot stores pop up across Ottawa", http://ottawacitizen.com/news/local-news/marijuana-dispensary-chains-move-into-ottawa-as-illegal-pot-stores-pop-up-across-town (Ottawa Citizen, Ottawa: 7 July 2016

[106] Andre Bourque, "Why Now Is the Perfect Time to Invest in Cannabis Edibles", https://merryjane.com/culture/why-now-is-the-perfect-time-to-invest-in-cannabis-edibles (Merry Jane: 17 January 2017).

[107] Debra Borchardt, "Cannabis Shoppers Come for One Thing, But Leave with Impulse Buys", https://www.forbes.com/sites/debraborchardt/2017/03/03/cannabis-shoppers-come-for-one-thing-but-leave-with-impulse-buys/2/#73bfc055fa67 (Forbes: 3 March 2017).

[108] Ibid.

[109] Anna Wilcox, "What to Know About Dosing, Potency, and Labeling", https://www.leafly.com/news/cannabis-101/medibles-101-everything-youve-ever-wanted-to-know-about-edibles (Leafly: 5 December 2013).

[110] Solomon Israel, "Despite special regulations, entrepreneurs hope to take bite of CANADA's marijuana edibles market", http://www.cbc.ca/news/business/Canada-legalization-marijuana-edibles-1.4079341 (CBC News, Toronto: 23 April 2017).

[111] Maureen Dowd, "Don't Harsh Our Mellow, Dude", https://www.nytimes.com/2014/06/04/opinion/dowd-dont-harsh-our-mellow-dude.html (The New York Times: 3 June 2014).

[112] Patrick Cain, *"Digesting legal weed: The hidden risks of eating marijuana"*, *http://globalnews.ca/news/3015394/digesting-legal-weed-the-hidden-risks-of-eating-marijuana/ (Global News, Toronto, a division of Corus*

Entertainment Inc.: 16 October 2016).

[113] Ibid.

[114] Ibid.

[115] Rosalina Nieves, "Chef brings cannabis to the dinner table, http://www.cnn.com/2016/11/08/health/herbal-chef-marijuana-dinners/index.html (CNN: 9 November 2016).

[116] Mitchell Hartman, "Does McDonald's have too many items on the menu?", https://www.marketplace.org/2013/05/23/business/food-and-drink/does-mcdonalds-have-too-many-items-menu (Marketplace: 23 May 2013).

[117] Sharon Fuller and Douglas Brown, How to Open a Financially Successful Bakery (Atlantic Publishing Group, Florida: 2004) p. 138.

[118] Leslie Jordan Clary, "What's Your Niche? Specialization in the Cannabis Industry", https://www.ganjapreneur.com/whats-niche-specialization-cannabis-industry/ (Ganjapreneur: 24 September 2014).

[119] Patrick Cain, "Legal pot in Canada could sell for $5 a gram — or less", http://globalnews.ca/news/3070170/legal-pot-could-sell-for-5-a-gram-or-less/ (*Global News, Toronto, a division of Corus Entertainment Inc.*: November 20, 2016).

[120] Ibid.

[121] Adrian Sedlin, "Here's what makes our marijuana 'top shelf' – and worth a 25% premium", https://www.cnbc.com/2017/08/08/what-makes-our-luxury-marijuana-worth-25-percent-more-ceo-commentary.html (CNBC: 8 August 2017).

[122] Jeff Grissler, Marijuana Business (2015), p.201.

[123] Julie Weed, "Cannabis CEOs Advise Aspiring Weed Entrepreneurs on Rules, Risks and Capital Needs," https://www.forbes.com/sites/julieweed/2017/04/10/cannabis-ceos-advise-would-be-weed-entrepreneurs-on-evaluating-rules-risks-and-capital-needs/#4e8085c395b3 (Forbes: 10 April 2017).

[124] Chad Finkelstein, "Here's how cannabis dispensaries could affect restaurants, inside and out",

http://www.nationalpost.com/here+cannabis+dispensaries+could+affect+re staurants+inside/13460926/story.html (National Post, Toronto: 20 June 2017).

125 Bulbulyan Consulting Group, 2015, infographic designed by Mad Fish Digital. Source: NBC News, Marijuana Policy Project, Denver Post, US News & World Report, US Department of Justice.

126 Chad Finkelstein, "Here's how cannabis dispensaries could affect restaurants, inside and out", http://www.nationalpost.com/here+cannabis+dispensaries+could+affect+re staurants+inside/13460926/story.html (National Post, Toronto: 20 June 2017).

127 Ibid.

128 Michael Mayes, "How to Design a Dispensary", http://quantum9.net/how-to-design-a-dispensary (Quantum 9: February 8, 2017).

129 Shan Li, "Marijuana shops are trying to look like the Apple store", http://www.latimes.com/business/la-fi-fancy-pot-shops-20161230-story.html (Los Angeles Times: 16 Jan 2017).

130 Ibid.

131 Ibid.

132 Ibid.

133 Leslie Jordan Clary, "What's Your Niche? Specialization in the Cannabis Industry", https://www.ganjapreneur.com/whats-niche-specialization-cannabis-industry/ (Ganjapreneur: 24 September 2014).

134 Randi Wooten, "Ask a Budtender: What Makes for Good Cannabis Packaging?", https://www.leafly.com/news/industry/ask-a-budtender-marijuana-packaging (Leafly. retrieved July 2017).

135 Julie Weed, "Cannabis CEOs Advise Aspiring Weed Entrepreneurs on Rules, Risks and Capital Needs," https://www.forbes.com/sites/julieweed/2017/04/10/cannabis-ceos-advise-would-be-weed-entrepreneurs-on-evaluating-rules-risks-and-capital-

needs/#4e8085c395b3 (Forbes: 10 April 2017).

[136] Tony Dokoupil and Bill Briggs, "Robber gangs terrorize Colorado pot shops", https://www.cnbc.com/2014/02/05/robber-gangs-terrorize-colorado-pot-shops.html (NBC News: 5 February 2014).

[137] Lauren Pelley, "Violent Toronto pot dispensary robberies often unreported, police say", http://www.cbc.ca/news/canada/toronto/marijuana-dispensary-robberies-1.3947761 (CBC news, Toronto: 23 January 2017).

[138] Bulbulyan Consulting Group, 2015, infographic designed by Mad Fish Digital. Source: NBC News, Marijuana Policy Project, Denver Post, US News & World Report, US Department of Justice.

[139] Ibid.

[140] Siva, "Making Security a Part of Your Medical Cannabis Business Plan", http://www.sivallc.com/making-security-part-medical-cannabis-business-plan/ (Siva: read August 2017).

[141] Amanda Pfeffer, "Police warn organized crime, including the Hells Angels, has infiltrated the medical marijuana market", http://www.cbc.ca/news/canada/ottawa/police-warn-organized-crime-including-the-hells-angels-has-infiltrated-the-medical-marijuana-market-1.4067112 (CBC News: 13 April 2017).

[142] NCV Newswire, "Bedrocan Canada Offers $5 per Gram Medical Cannabis Pricing on all Products", https://www.newcannabisventures.com/bedrocan-5-dollars-per-gram/ (New Cannabis Ventures: 25 January 2016).

[143] Martin Patriquin, "Is Canada Ready for Legal Marijuana? ", https://www.nytimes.com/2017/08/24/opinion/canada-legalize-marijuana.html (The New York Times: 24 August 2017).

[144] Richard Hollinger, National Retail Security Survey, https://nrf.com/system/tdf/Documents/retail%20library/NRF_2016_NRSS_restricted-rev.pdf?file=1&title=National%20Retail%20Security%20Survey%202016 (University of Florida: 2009) pg. 9.

[145] Helen Cousins, "Common Accounting Mistakes That Can Cause Serious Trouble", http://tweakyourbiz.com/finance/2013/01/08/common-accounting-mistakes-that-can-cause-serious-trouble (Tweak Your Biz: 8 September 2013).

146 Audrey McAvoy, "Hawaii to be first state where all cannabis dispensaries provide cashless sales", http://www.thecannabist.co/2017/09/13/hawaii-cashless-marijuana-sales/87973/ (The Cannabist: 13 September 2017).

147 Lissa Townsend Rodgers, "Cybersecurity and Cannabis", http://vegasseven.com/2017/01/18/cybersecurity-and-cannabis (Vegas Seven 18 January 2017).

148 Amy O'Connor, "High on Marijuana Insurance", http://www.insurancejournal.com/magazines/features/2014/09/08/339286.htm (Insurance Journal: 8 September 2014).

149 MMD Insurance, "MMD Offers Product Liability Coverage for Medical Cannabis Firms", http://www.insurancejournal.com/news/national/2010/11/01/114512.htm (Insurance Journal: 1 November 2010).

150 Julie Weed, "Cannabis CEOs Advise Aspiring Weed Entrepreneurs on Rules, Risks and Capital Needs," https://www.forbes.com/sites/julieweed/2017/04/10/cannabis-ceos-advise-would-be-weed-entrepreneurs-on-evaluating-rules-risks-and-capital-needs/#4e8085c395b3 (Forbes: 10 April 2017).

151 Yvonne Zacharias, "Vancouver pot seller's criminal past, and more evidence of Hells Angels in dispensary business, alleged in court documents" , ", http://www.vancouversun.com/health/Vancouver+seller+criminal+past+more+evidence+Hells+Angels+dispensary+business+alleged+court/11297166/story.html (Vancouver Sun, Vancouver: 17 August 2015).

152 Laura Kane, "Canadians with marijuana convictions call on Trudeau to offer pardons", http://www.cbc.ca/news/politics/marijuana-convictions-justin-trudeau-legalization-1.3377056 (22 December 2015).

153 Ibid.

154 Catherine Morisset, "Employment 1010: Background Checks", https://www.marijuanaventure.com/employment-101-background-checks/ (Marijuana Venture: 25 November 2016).

155 CharTec, "Cost of Replacing an Employee", https://chartec.net/cost-of-

replacing-an-employee (Chartec.net: retrieved July 2017).

[156] Leafly Staff, "Part 2, How to Get Hired as a Budtender ",
https://www.leafly.com/news/industry/how-to-get-hired-to-work-in-the-medical-cannabis-industry-part-2 (Leafly, retrieved July 2017).

[157] Paul Gerber, "Top Three Criminal Record Check Recommended
Practices", https://www.cannabisbusinessexecutive.com/2016/05/top-three-criminal-record-check-recommended-practices (Cannabis Business Executive: 17 May 2016).

[158] Ibid

[159] Mikal E. Belicove, "The 10 Dos and Don'ts of Conducting Employee
Background Checks",
https://www.forbes.com/sites/mikalbelicove/2012/10/26/the-10-dos-and-donts-o-conducting-employee-background-checks/#5f3a65ff4e2b (Forbes:
26 October 2012).

[160] CFIB, "Pre-employment screening: Conducting criminal background
checks", http://www.cfib-fcei.ca/english/article/5968-pre-employment-screening-conducting-criminal-background-checks.html (Canadian Federation of Independent Business: read August 2017).

[161] Mikal E. Belicove, "The 10 Dos and Don'ts of Conducting Employee
Background Checks",
https://www.forbes.com/sites/mikalbelicove/2012/10/26/the-10-dos-and-donts-o-conducting-employee-background-checks/#5f3a65ff4e2b (Forbes:
26 October 2012).

[162] Catherine Morisset, "Employment 1010: Background Checks",
https://www.marijuanaventure.com/employment-101-background-checks/
(Marijuana Venture: 25 November 2016).

[163] Paul Gerber, "Top Three Criminal Record Check Recommended
Practices", https://www.cannabisbusinessexecutive.com/2016/05/top-three-criminal-record-check-recommended-practices (Cannabis Business Executive: 17 May 2016).

[164] Mikal E. Belicove, "The 10 Dos and Don'ts of Conducting Employee
Background Checks",
https://www.forbes.com/sites/mikalbelicove/2012/10/26/the-10-dos-and-donts-o-conducting-employee-background-checks/#5f3a65ff4e2b (Forbes:
26 October 2012).

165 Lisa Rough, "5 Mistakes to Avoid When Hiring a Budtender", https://www.leafly.com/news/industry/5-mistakes-avoid-hiring-budtender (Leafly: 1 February 2017).

166 The Stranger, "The Stranger's Guide to Every Recreational Weed Store in Seattle", http://www.thestranger.com/weed/2016/11/16/24677904/the-strangers-guide-to-every-recreational-weed-store-in-seattle (The Stranger: 16 November 2016).

167 Amy Gallo, "The Value of Keeping the Right Customers", https://hbr.org/2014/10/the-value-of-keeping-the-right-customers (Harvard Business Review: 29 October 2014).

168 Nielsen Newswire, "Consumer Trust in Online, Social and Mobile Advertising Grows", http://www.nielsen.com/us/en/insights/news/2012/consumer-trust-in-online-social-and-mobile-advertising-grows.html (10 April 2012).

169 Amanda Stillwagon, "Did You Know: A 5percent Increase in Retention Increases Profits by Up to 95 percent", https://smallbiztrends.com/2014/09/increase-in-customer-retention-increases-profits.html (Small Business Trends: 11 September 2014).

170 Julie Weed, "Best Practices: Cannabis Executives Share Social Media Advice," https://www.forbes.com/sites/julieweed/2017/07/16/best-practices-cannabis-executives-share-social-media-advice/#77b578c32e72 (Forbes: 16 July 2017).

171 Ibid.

172 Ibid.

173 Keith Wagstaff, "The Average American Spends 40 Minutes a Day on Facebook", http://www.nbcnews.com/tech/social-media/average-american-spends-40-minutes-day-facebook-n164046 (24 NBC News: July 2014).

174 Jay Baer, "11 Shocking New Social Media Statistics in America", http://www.convinceandconvert.com/social-media-research/11-shocking-new-social-media-statistics-in-america (Convince & Convert: retrieved July 2017).

[175] Leafly Staff, "Part 4, Social Media Marketing Strategies ",
https://www.leafly.com/news/industry/how-to-market-your-cannabis-business-part-4-social-media-marketin (Leafly, retrieved July 2017).

[176] Julie Weed, "Best Practices: Cannabis Executives Share Social Media Advice," https://www.forbes.com/sites/julieweed/2017/07/16/best-practices-cannabis-executives-share-social-media-advice/#77b578c32e72 (Forbes: 16 July 2017).

[177] Leafly Staff, "Part 4, Social Media Marketing Strategies ",
https://www.leafly.com/news/industry/how-to-market-your-cannabis-business-part-4-social-media-marketin (Leafly, retrieved July 2017).

[178] Ibid.

[179] Ibid.

[180] Ibid.

[181] Ibid.

[182] Jeffrey Zwelling, "Pinterest drives more revenue per click than Twitter or Facebook", http://venturebeat.com/2012/04/09/pinterest-drives-more-revenue-per-click-than-twitter-or-facebook/. (VentureBeat: 9 April 2012).

[183] Ibid.

[184] Ibid.

[185] Julie Weed, "Cannabis CEOs Advise Aspiring Weed Entrepreneurs on Rules, Risks and Capital Needs,"
https://www.forbes.com/sites/julieweed/2017/04/10/cannabis-ceos-advise-would-be-weed-entrepreneurs-on-evaluating-rules-risks-and-capital-needs/#4e8085c395b3 (Forbes: 10 April 2017).

[186] Aaron Apple, "Email Marketing Ideas for Cannabis Companies",
https://www.ganjapreneur.com/email-marketing-ideas-cannabis-dispensaries/ (Ganjapreneur: 17 October 2016).

[187] Matt Ferner, "Marijuana Ads Banned On Google, Facebook and Twitter",
http://www.huffingtonpost.ca/entry/google-facebook-ban-marijuana_n_4646916 (The Huffington Post: 22 Jan 2014)

[188] Ibid.

[189] Ibid.

[190] Debra Borchardt, "CanPay Debuts First Legitimate Debit Payment System for Cannabis Purchases", https://www.forbes.com/sites/debraborchardt/2016/11/17/1035/#4c1961de 3369 (Forbes: 17 November 2016).

[191] Matt Ferner, "High-Tech Marijuana Tracking System Introduced in Colorado", http://www.huffingtonpost.ca/entry/marijuana-tracking_n_4433503 (Huffington Post: 12 December 2013).

[192] Alexandra Posadzki, "2 of Canada's top banks back away from marijuana industry", http://www.cbc.ca/news/business/banks-marijuana-business-1.3757927 (The Canadian Press: 12 September 2016).

[193] Ibid.

[194] Julie Weed, "Behind the Scenes at Three Luxury Pot Shops That Are Hiring," https://www.forbes.com/sites/julieweed/2017/07/10/behind-the-scenes-at-three-luxury-pot-shops-theyre-gorgeous-and-theyre-hiring/#595fbba96651 (Forbes: 10 April 2017).

[195] Debra Borchardt, "CanPay Debuts First Legitimate Debit Payment System for Cannabis Purchases", https://www.forbes.com/sites/debraborchardt/2016/11/17/1035/#4c1961de 3369 (Forbes: 17 November 2016).

[196] Ibid.

[197] Julie Weed, "BioTrackTHC Helps Marijuana Businesses Track Inventory and Comply with Regulations", https://www.forbes.com/sites/julieweed/2016/02/13/biotrackthc-helps-marijuana-businesses-track-it-all-from-seed-to-sale/#51917b266077 (13 February 2016).

[198] Lisa Rough, "6 Strategies for Selling Excess Cannabis Product Inventory", https://www.leafly.com/news/industry/6-strategies-selling-excess-cannabis-product-inventory (Leafly: read August 2017).

[199] Sharon Fuller and Douglas Brown, How to Open a Financially Successful Bakery (Atlantic Publishing Group, Florida: 2004) p. 236.

[200] Julie Weed, "Cannabis CEOs Advise Aspiring Weed Entrepreneurs on Rules, Risks and Capital Needs," https://www.forbes.com/sites/julieweed/2017/04/10/cannabis-ceos-advise-would-be-weed-entrepreneurs-on-evaluating-rules-risks-and-capital-needs/#4e8085c395b3 (Forbes: 10 April 2017).

[201] ESOP Advisory Group, "The Advantages of ESOP Financing", http://www.esopadvisorsgroup.com/home.html (ESOP Advisory Group, Issue Brief # 6: 18 July 2003). p. 5.

Made in the USA
Middletown, DE
12 October 2021

50194389R00149